Job Hunting
in the
21st Century

Exploding the Myths,
Exploring the Realities

Job Hunting
in the
21st Century

Exploding the Myths,
Exploring the Realities

Carol A. Hacker

S$_L^t$

St. Lucie Press

Boca Raton　London　New York　Washington, D.C.

Library of Congress Cataloging-in-Publication Data

Hacker, Carol A.
    Job hunting in the 21st century : exploding the myths, exploring the realities / Carol A. Hacker
        p. cm.
    Includes bibliographical references and index.
    ISBN 1-57444-242-2 (soft)
    1. Job hunting. I. Title. II. Title: Job hunting in the twenty-first century
HF5382.7.H32   1999
650.14—dc21

                                              98-48948
                                                  CIP

Dedication

For Samantha W. Renfro, Director of MBA Career Services,
Goizueta Business School of Emory University, her staff, and the
men and women in the MBA program who have taught me more than
you will ever know about life, business, and friendships.

Contents

PART II—THE CAMPAIGN

Myths…

PART III—THE INTERVIEW AND BEYOND

Myths...

Preface

Job hunters usually fall into one of three major categories: (1) those just entering the job market after graduation; (2) those currently jobless who had full-time employment previously; and (3) those who are employed but looking for a different job. The last category includes people seeking new jobs in the same career field for more money, career advancement, or personal fulfillment as well as those pursuing a change in careers.

This book covers myths that affect job seekers in all three categories.

There are numerous misconceptions associated with career choices, changes, and adjustments—misconceptions that have sabotaged the attempts of many people. I've identified the most common myths that concern job seekers, both the novice and the experienced. I've used easy-to-understand-and-apply language and concepts to explain the realities. I've also interviewed job hunters like you, as well as employers looking for new employees.

Job Hunting in the 21st Century: Exploding the Myths, Exploring the Realities offers practical advice in the following areas:

1. Defining a career goal
2. Preparing or updating a resume
3. Preparing a customized cover letter
4. Locating job opportunities
5. Researching a company
6. Choosing the best employment agency
7. Preparing for pre-employment tests
8. Handling tough interview questions
9. The importance of references
10. Negotiating salary and benefits

Don't let the myths cloud your thinking and prevent you from approaching the realities with common sense and a belief that you will succeed. Recognizing and exploding a myth while understanding and exploring the reality is the first step to a successful job search.

Acknowledgments

Countless people have contributed to the success of this book: Thank you to Drew Gierman, Editor and Acting Publisher, St. Lucie Press Business Division, for believing in me once again; Judy Rogers, dear friend and editor, for your superb expertise and encouragement; Christine Winter for your conscientious approach to editing and attention to detail; and Kathie Stebick, an invaluable supporter and treasured friend.

Special thanks to Bill and Cher Holton for your continuing support and creative suggestions. Thanks to Rod Kennedy, Ph.D. for all of your great ideas. Your many years of practical experience and career counseling perspective helped make this book a success.

Words don't seem like enough to thank Bill Coffman. You are a kind friend and incredible leader. You've helped me through the most difficult time in my life and inspired me to finish this book. Thank you.

Thanks to Woodrow McKay, Richard Stanford, and Bill McKoy, members of the Atlanta Writers Club and my editorial group. You are all terrific and gave so generously of yourselves in helping me with the manuscript. I appreciate your candid input.

Dorothy Einstein, you're a wonderful friend. Thank you for the opportunity to spend quiet time at your lovely home to work on this book.

Thanks to all the people who were interviewed for the book who have allowed me to share your private and personal successes and failures. You have helped others to help themselves because of your honesty. You are:

Kathryn Allen	Sue Beal	Tim Bond
Todd Ashland	Tim Blaylock	Ross Bowin
Natalie Barnes	Ted Bock	Malcolm Brown

Mark Canosa
Glen Christiansen
Ellen Marie Chung
Candy Clarke
Mike Conner
Alice Dalton
Jeannie Dalton
Hank Drew
Craig Espinoza
Taylor Gibbs
Al Givens
Betsy Glade
Shirley Grimm
Jenny Hall
Tami Harmmond
Debbie Hart
Tonya Hinkleman
Laura Hinton
Patrick Hodges
Andrew Holmes
Louise Hopper

Lois Hunt
Jim Hunter
Reginald Johnson
Pete Kelley
Sally Kerner
Rick Kryzinski
Karl Magnusen, Ph.D.
Becky Marist
Jay Marnie
Bob Mathis
Troy Maysick
Derick Moeller
Paige O'Conner
Helen Overton
Sandra Owens
Eleanor Parker-Jones
Edna Peoples
Ann Raporpart
Frank Reuter
Tina Ann Rubin
Herbert Sanders

Albert Santiago
Lyle Sawyer
Brenda Sax
Ed Scranton
Sue Shansky
T.J. Sinclair
Peter Stanford
Claude Stephens
Wanda Stone
Eddie Strauss
Eva Taglienta
Bob Tanner
Ralph Timmons
Tim Thomas
Ted Trindle
Regina Tully
Erin Turner
Dean Williams, M.D.
Kenneth Wilkins
Bill Wyatt
Mary Lou Yoder

The Author

Carol A. Hacker is an educator, speaker, and the founder of Carol A. Hacker & Associates, one of the country's foremost skill-building enterprises on human resource management. For more than two decades she has been a significant voice in front-line and corporate human resource management to Fortune 500 companies as well as small businesses. With hands-on experience in managing a wide variety of public, private, and nonprofit projects, her client list spans North America and Europe.

Carol is a graduate of the University of Wisconsin, where she earned a B.S. and M.S. with honors. Prior to starting her own firm in January 1989, she held a number of management positions, including that of Director of Human Resources for the North American division of Bahlsen Inc., a European manufacturer.

She is the author of *Hiring Top Performers—350 Great Interview Questions for People Who Need People* (1998, revised), *The High Cost of Low Morale ... and what to do about it* (St. Lucie Press, 1997), *The Costs of Bad Hiring Decisions & How to Avoid Them, 2nd Edition* (St. Lucie Press, 1999), and dozens of published articles.

She speaks for professional and trade associations, as well as for private corporations and government agencies. Her motivational presentations are practical and positive. Her interactive workshops have helped thousands of managers become better leaders.

Carol is available to speak or to consult with organizations on the topics of selecting and keeping winning employees. For more information contact her at 770-410-0517, 209 Cutty Sark Way, Alpharetta, GA 30005.

Introduction

How will I find a job? How long will it take? Suppose no one will hire me. Will I join the ranks of the homeless? How will I pay my bills? What do I do now? If you're looking for a job, and your thoughts and feelings are similar to these, you're not alone.

Whether you're a new entry into the job market or you're jobless due to personal choice, downsizing, relocation, or being fired, the challenge is the same: you need to find a job. If you're looking for a job while employed, you face a slightly different challenge: you need to find a job that justifies the change.

If you're entering the job market after graduation from school, you face a new and exciting world of choices. Although most graduates have some experience working through summer jobs or part-time employment, it's a different situation when you're seeking a permanent career position.

If you're jobless due to termination (downsizing, layoffs, being fired) you probably were in shock when you got the word that you no longer had a job. You may have asked yourself, "Why me?" (There may not have been an answer then; there may never be an answer why it happened to you.) You may also have wondered, "Are former colleagues laughing behind my back?" You began to grieve. In your grief, you moved from shock to anger to denial and back again. You may have remained stuck in the grieving mode for many weeks or even months. But at some point you realized you had to begin a job search.

Perhaps you're jobless by choice. You hated your job, your boss, and the company. You couldn't stand it anymore, so you quit. Maybe you had second thoughts about your decision to resign, but it was too late to turn back. You had no alternative but to follow through with your decision. Even if you initially felt relief at leaving and happy about the action you took, now you have to find another job.

If you're among those who are employed but seeking a job or career change, you may find yourself filled with doubt as to the wisdom of what you're doing. Even if you're sure you're pursuing the right course, you may have questions about how the job search process has changed.

To make matters worse, you've got competition. Reorganizations of all types have flooded the marketplace with qualified, as well as not-so-qualified, job hunters. The focus in *Job Hunting in the 21st Century: Exploding the Myths, Exploring the Realities* is on helping you beat the competition.

One major difference between today's job market and that of the past is the change in the employment process. For example, 30 years ago when you accepted a job offer, you usually expected to spend your entire working life with the same employer. If you worked hard and remained loyal, the organization would usually provide rewards.

By the mid-1970s, trends began to shift. You valued job security, but discovered that your employer had other plans. Layoffs, not uncommon by today's standards, became a terrible new reality. Workers asked, "What happened to the belief that employees are an organization's most valuable asset?"

The 1980s and 1990s brought more change. Mergers and acquisitions were in vogue and more and more people lost their jobs. Those who escaped layoff often suffered "survivor sickness," the symptoms of which include anger, hurt, fear, guilt, and sadness. In addition, advances in technology changed job performance expectations and increased the pressure on workers to stay abreast of current conditions.

As you approach the 21st century, it's time to take a fresh look at how you're competing. Your strategy for finding that first job, dealing with job loss, or changing careers can make the difference in how fast you get the job offer you want.

Read this book carefully. See if some of the myths are ones you believe. Take notes as you read. Re-read chapters that particularly apply to you. Don't let the myths cloud your thinking. Accept the realities. Let these suggestions help you develop an action plan for a successful journey to a new job. Sell yourself into the job of your choice, not just whatever happens to come along.

GET STARTED

Employers recruit energy, enthusiasm, inventiveness, and desire. Candidates are valuable to companies because of the skills they hold that can produce results. However, if your career is off track, you probably don't have any of these things to offer. Therefore, your job search starts with *you* and a self-assessment regarding your career choice.

Separating career-related myths from realities is essential for effective career planning and decision making. Many job seekers don't realize that accepting these myths as realities can prevent them from getting what they want from their careers, both emotionally and financially. Consequently, they mismanage their careers, make strategic errors, and eventually face the unhappy realization that they're working in a job that provides only minimal satisfaction.

Until you can answer the question, "What do I want to do?" you'll probably have a tough time getting your job search off the ground. Part I covers the most common career planning myths and offers practical suggestions on how to overcome them.

Once you've decided what direction you want to take, it's time to start writing. The purpose of the resume and cover letter is to describe your skills and capabilities so accurately and persuasively that you get invitations for interviews. Keep in mind that resumes don't get jobs; interviews do. Use your resume to help you get the first interview. Tailor it to fit the job and organization you want to join.

In addition, keep in mind that cover letters are more than just wrapping paper for your resume. They're your first opportunity to tell the reader why you're the best person for the job. If you understand the importance of a well-written cover letter, your resume will get the kind of notice you're hoping for. An invitation for a personal interview gives you the chance to convince the hiring manager that you can and will do the job, as well as be a perfect fit.

Understanding the myths/realities in Part I can help you as you develop a plan for your initial approach to contacting prospective employers.

Some of the most common myths concerning starting a job search are:

1. If I'm unemployed, employers will think I'm a loser.
2. Most successful people had a good idea early in life what kind of careers they wanted.
3. A good way to find a new career is by the process of elimination.
4. Changing careers is the best solution to a bad job.
5. Changing careers is easy as long as you know what you want to do.
6. If you have enough interest in a particular career, you'll be successful.
7. Resumes get jobs.
8. Resumes should always include a job objective.
9. It's important to include on your resume every job you've ever held.
10. It's a good idea to include a photograph with your resume.
11. Functional resumes aren't as effective as chronological resumes.
12. The more information you have on your resume, the better.
13. Including your age, race, marital status, height, weight, and religion on your resume gives it a personal touch.
14. It's a good strategy to list references on your resume.
15. Plain resumes don't get fancy job offers.
16. Mass mailing resumes is an effective job-search strategy.
17. The best way to send a resume is by mail or fax.
18. It's acceptable not to use a cover letter with your resume.
19. A handwritten cover letter conveys a feeling of warmth.
20. Generic, mass-produced cover letters are effective for certain positions.
21. Unusual-looking cover letters and resumes make you stand out.

Myth #1

If I'm unemployed, employers will think I'm a loser.

Reality

Being unemployed is a stigma only if you allow it to be.

Discussion

Unemployment is an unfortunate fact of life. However, don't let it destroy your sense of self-worth. From time to time, talented people sometimes find themselves unemployed. Recruiters and hiring managers understand this. Whether you were laid off, terminated, or quit, you still have the same goal—find another job. That's difficult to do if you have "loser" written on your face.

For example, Tami Harmmond had this to say about her experience after losing a job: "I was laid off in February but didn't start looking for another job until June. I felt embarrassed, and that was a mistake. I had lots of excuses for why I wasn't actively looking. I guess I was afraid to try and fail. It wasn't until after I started interviewing that I realized being unemployed is nothing to be ashamed of."

Reginald Johnson, a recruiter with a national employment agency, had this to say: "Most people change jobs several times during their careers. Some will quit; others will be laid off or fired. However, when you're unemployed, you have to put forth your best effort or you run the risk that interviewers will see you as someone who's depressed, angry, and not ready for another job. I'm reminded of a woman who was looking for work. When she answered the telephone she did so with a tone of voice that sounded annoyed and emphasized the 'HELL' in the word 'hello.' No employer in his or her right mind would be interested in someone with her attitude. Most businesses already have enough problem employees without adding another one to the payroll."

Here are some tips to help you remain positive even when you don't feel motivated to find another job:

1. Get started immediately. The sooner you start your search, the better.
2. Stick to a plan. Set goals, write them down, and follow through.
3. Keep a journal of your activities. Write in it every day. At the end of the week, review it and see how much you've done.
4. Take an occasional break from your job search. Relax; do something you enjoy.
5. Associate with positive people. Negative people will drag you down.
6. Take a class; learn a new skill or enhance old skills.

Remember that employers need you as much as you need them. View yourself as a provider of service, and someone who has the capability to apply your knowledge and expertise to a variety of jobs. You're not a loser—you're just a person looking for the right job.

Myth #2

Most successful people had a good idea early in life what kind of careers they wanted.

Reality

Few people have a clear vision of what they expect to be doing 5 or 10 years in the future.

Discussion

Just because you didn't see your career path clearly when you were in junior high school doesn't doom you to failure. Today people often have several careers over the course of their working years.

Many adults that are perceived as successful ended up in their careers by default. In reality they've never been truly happy with their career decisions. There are also successful people who lacked career direction at some point in their lives but learned how to plan and set goals.

Maybe you've been following someone else's choice for your career. A well-meaning parent or relative may have encouraged you to get into a profession he or she considered practical but that you weren't interested in and have grown to dislike more and more over time.

Maybe you chose a career because someone you admired worked in that field, but you didn't consider whether such a choice would meet your personal and individual needs.

People develop at different rates. Sometimes people spend years in jobs before they decide to venture into something else. People also change over time; the job that fulfilled an individual 10 years ago may leave him or her feeling bored and restless today.

Whether you're preparing to enter the job market but are unsure about what kind of work you'd like, or just feel it's time to make a change, ask yourself these questions:

- *What can I do?* For example:

    What special skills/knowledge do I use to perform my job duties?

    How effective am I as a leader of others?

    Am I willing to be assertive when needed?

    Does being assertive make me uncomfortable?

    What special skills do I have that I don't currently use?

    Am I free to travel?

- *What do I want to do?* For example:

    What did/do I like most about my previous/current job?

    What was my favorite project?

    What would I like to do more of in my next job?

    Would I prefer working alone or as part of a group/team?

    Would I be willing to take classes to acquire new skills?

    Do I want to be in a position of authority, or would I be happy as a follower?

    Do I have special interests or hobbies that I'd like to use in my job?

    Would I be willing to relocate?

Take time to answer the questions in each category. You may be able to do many things well, but have *interest* in only a few. When developing your career plans, consider jobs that include the things you enjoy doing as well as what you're able to do. The best job for you should combine both elements.

How well you'll fit into a job depends on how compatible you are with the culture of the hiring organization.

Example: Sue Shansky, a 36-year-old secretary, wanted a new career. She decided these things about herself:

- I have an aptitude for writing. *(can do)*
- I feel comfortable expressing myself orally. *(can do)*
- I like to analyze information. (*can do* and *want to do*)
- I like reporting. *(want to do)*
- I enjoy meeting new people. *(want to do)*

These statements suggested that she explore occupations where she could use her writing and interpersonal skills. Shansky decided to pursue a career as a newspaper reporter or communications specialist in the mobile communications industry. She had worked as a secretary in this field for 12 years and understood the business.

She discussed her career plans with her supervisor and completed her B.S. degree in night school. When a position became available she applied and was promoted to Communications Coordinator. Today, she works on the company newsletter and prepares written announcements for distribution to employees. She interacts with people at all levels in the company.

Shansky successfully achieved her goal because she decided what she wanted to do and developed a plan to get there.

Every individual has a wide array of abilities and talents. Each person has several career possibilities, all of which may be equally satisfying. Different careers present different degrees of challenge.

Today we have five times the job diversification that we had only 10 years ago. We can expect this variety to continue expanding in the coming years. Even those people who make a definite career choice early on may find themselves working in many different jobs during their lifetime.

Myth #3

A good way to find a new career is by the process of elimination.

Reality

This method tends to be time-consuming and impractical. Consider the process of self-discovery instead.

Discussion

Whether you're jobless and are thinking about a new career, or employed but feel you're at the point where you're ready to try something new, a number of vocational tests are available to help you. There are many tests to choose from, but keep in mind that no one test can determine exactly what you do best. It's usually advisable to take a combination of tests and interest surveys to determine the direction that's right for you. While you can self-administer and score some tests, you may need professional interpretation for others.

Some of the most popular career abilities tests available are:

- *COPES—Career Occupational Placement Evaluation Survey:* Helps assess your values and motivations and measures problem-solving skills.

- *CAPS—Career Ability Placement Survey:* Provides an assessment of occupational skills and can help you decide which areas you may want to develop.

- *CASI—Career Attitudes and Strategies Inventory: An Inventory for Understanding Adult Careers:* Provides a career check-up for employed and unemployed adults in a self-administered and self-scored format.

- *CRIS—Coping Resources Inventory for Stress:* Measures, among other things, how you handle stress on the job.

- *CPI—California Psychological Inventory:* Assesses leadership and management capabilities.

- *DAT for PCA—Differential Aptitude Tests for Personnel and Career Assessment:* Determines how likely you are to succeed in eight aptitude areas that relate to successful job performance.

- *Meyers–Briggs Type Indicator:* Assesses your personality type based on eight factors. Can help you define the type of work environment where you'll best fit.

- *SDS—Self Directed Search:* Helps you compile a profile of behaviors and characteristics that can be compared to occupational listings in the Occupations Finder and Career Options Finder categorized by Holland's personality types.

- *Strong Interest Inventory:* Compares your answers to a series of questions with those of thousands of individuals in a variety of occupations.

Some tests are designed for use at home. You can find others at many high schools and college career centers. Some organizations sell their test instruments only to counselors or psychologists.

Regardless of where and how you use an assessment tool, keep in mind that these instruments provide information you may use as guidance in seeking a new career direction. Although you still have to consider many other factors (ability, family needs, expectations), you can use these vocational tests to provide fresh insight as you decide which job best fits your personality and ambitions.

In the case of one executive who wanted to change jobs, the information he gathered from the tests helped him evaluate a possible career change. When he learned more about his personality type and needs, he understood why he wasn't happy at his present job. The information also indicated he had the personality traits needed for the new career field in which he had an interest, and this gave him confidence to make a change.

There's one more aspect to self-discovery in addition to the practical application of tests and exercises. Do a little day dreaming. Maybe you so closely identify with your job that you're having a hard time thinking of yourself as separate from your job. You may never pursue your dream job, but thinking about it may give you clues concerning some of your hidden ambitions.

Suppose, for example, you could have any job you wanted and succeed at it. What would you do? Where would you like to do it? Imagine how you'd spend an average day in this dream job, what hours you'd work, with whom you would work, etc. Imagine the atmosphere at the job; would you want it to be casual, moderately structured, or somewhere in between? What is the most special part of the job? Then think about where you'd like to live as part of the dream. Are you willing to relocate to another part of the country or world?

The answers to your questions may give you some surprising insights into some things you weren't aware of about yourself. It may provide additional information to help you make your decision about a career change.

Myth #4

Changing careers is the best solution to a bad job.

Reality

A career change is *usually not* the solution to job problems.

Discussion

Before making a decision to change careers because you feel discontented or have difficulties on the job, consider this question carefully: *"Do you know what went wrong or why you're unhappy with your present career?"*

Example: Ellen Marie Chung wants a career change because she can't find a job in her field. Ted Trindle disagrees with the policies of his employer. Mike Conner can't tolerate the people he works with and has a reputation for having an attitude problem. All three believe a career change will solve their problems.

Before you make a decision as major as pursuing a new career, take time to sort through your reasons for taking this step.

In Chung's case, she could consider another area of employment within her career field. Many skills will transfer from one area to another within the same field. For example, a senior medical technician decided to make a change, and ended up taking a position as a medical recruiter. His knowledge of the medical field helped him make the move.

Often people become so focused on a particular job within a career field that they fail to realize the wide range of jobs available to them, or to understand that their skills and training will transfer to another job.

As always, of course, job hunters must examine whether there is some underlying reason why they're not getting job offers in their career field. If they're making basic job hunting mistakes, changing careers probably won't solve the problem. They'll simply be jobless in a different field.

In the case of Trindle and Conner, they might want to consider some important questions before making a change:

- Do I have frequent disputes with fellow employees?
- Have I ever been fired as a result of a personality conflict with my supervisor or another employee?
- Do I feel I'm in a "dead-end" job?
- Do I feel my abilities far outweigh the responsibilities of my job?
- Do I feel inadequately compensated for what I do?
- Do I feel that my supervisor never gives me credit for my efforts?
- Do I believe that the company mistreats its employees?
- Does my work bore me? Why?
- Does life in general bore me? Why?
- Would I accept almost any other job offer just to get out of the job I have?
- Is there any one aspect of my present career (such as travel) that I particularly like or dislike? Why?
- Have I discussed my concerns with my supervisor?
- Do I consider my job "beneath" me?
- What would I need in a job in order to feel successful?
- What have I done in the way of professional development?
- Have I encountered similar problems or job dissatisfactions in other jobs I've held?

A career change is a serious decision. What's right for someone else may not be right for you. Carefully evaluate your reasons for the change. Consider asking family members and close friends for their opinions, but only if you want them to tell you the truth. You may also want to consult a professional career counselor before making your final decision.

Switching careers is not a guaranteed quick cure for unemployment or for unhappiness on the job.

Myth #5

Changing careers is easy as long as you know what you want to do.

Reality

It's not easy to make a change in jobs, much less a career.

Discussion

The media and current literature often treat career change as a simple process. In reality, the average person has many obstacles to overcome. These could include family concerns, personal issues, a need for more education, insufficient funds, inadequate work experience and skills, and/or lack of emotional support from family and friends.

If you're thinking about a career change, consider the following:

- Are you willing to make the commitment it takes to change careers?
- Have you thoroughly evaluated your present career?
- How well have you managed your career up until this point?
- Do you know why you want to make a career change?
- Have you thoroughly researched the new career you're considering?
- Will you need additional education?

17

- Do you have the financial resources to make a change?
- How do family members feel about the possible career change?

You may want to work with a career counselor as part of the change process. An impartial person can help you identify areas where you may encounter difficulties. Also consider using informational interviews to "test" your career choice before you make a decision.

Don't depend on headhunters and employment agencies to provide help; they usually don't want to work with people changing careers. Even if you have someone willing to serve as your mentor during the change process, you'll likely discover that finding a job in your new career field is something you'll have to do on your own.

In working out your decision to change careers, consider the change in terms of a three-stage event by writing down:

1. Your plan for the next year.
2. Goals you want to reach within the next 5 years.
3. Your long-term objective—where do you want to be by retirement age?

The people who are the most likely to make a *successful* career change have leadership skills, a variety of interests, and financial resources. They're also bursting with ideas and energy begging for release in a different vocational direction.

Example: Ross Bowin decided to change careers when he turned 50. He had worked on Wall Street for 25 years and was tired of his company, his supervisor, and his job. Bowin was financially secure and decided to pursue a career as a chef. Cooking had been a hobby for more than a decade. He enjoyed preparing elegant meals for family and friends. He considered his options and took a job as a chef at a private club.

"I've never been happier. The decision to make a career change at midlife was the right move for me. However, I had a plan before I quit my job as a stockbroker. I recommend that if you want to change careers you find out as much as possible about the career in which you're interested. Talk to people who do what you want to do. Ask them what they like best about their careers and what they would like to change. Listen. Take notes. Discuss what you learn with your family and maybe a few close friends. Make an informed decision, but don't expect everything to immediately fall into place. It takes time to make a major change like I did; it may not always work out like you anticipate."

Myth #6

If you have enough interest in a particular career, you'll be successful.

Reality

Just because you like what you're doing doesn't necessarily mean you'll succeed and make a living doing it.

Discussion

Keep in mind that *interests* and *aptitudes* are not the same. What you would like to do and what you have the skills to do may be two different things. For example, an interest may motivate you to want to become a professional tennis player. However, your interest may not be enough to compensate for deficiencies in ability or lack of aptitude for the game.

Even a combination of interest and aptitude doesn't always mean you'll enjoy doing something as a career. Having an interest and aptitude for mathematics, for example, doesn't necessarily mean you'll enjoy being a high school math teacher or engineer.

Example: Todd Ashland loved to play cards so he decided to become a card dealer in Las Vegas. He moved to Nevada, enrolled in a dealer school, and after graduation found a job in a nearby casino. He soon discovered that the job did not keep him challenged. In addition, he was sick from the smoke, tired of standing, and fed up with the clientele. His interest in cards wasn't enough to keep him motivated and satisfied with his new career.

Another consideration is how happy you'll be with your career choice if you don't produce enough income to cover your needs. If you have a true interest in a career field that offers primarily low-paying jobs, are you willing to adjust your standard of living to match your income? Some people would feel job satisfaction compensates for lower pay; others would not.

A very important consideration in the personality department is whether you're an extrovert or introvert. Extroverts want people around them; they get their energy from being with people. They often think out loud as they work toward solutions. Introverts derive most of their energy from their minds. They think things through silently. They would just as soon work alone as with others, and get tired when too many people are around them. Neither personality type is right or wrong. Most of us can act either way at times.

Example: Laura Hinton, administrative assistant, preferred working alone. Her supervisor was frequently out of town and depended on her to keep things running smoothly at the office. She enjoyed spending hours at her desk organizing and working on special projects. Laura didn't feel a need for the social contact of a larger, multi-employee office. On the weekends, however, she enjoyed attending social gatherings or entertaining friends and family at her home. Laura was basically an introvert at work and an extrovert at play.

When it comes to work, each individual prefers one or the other method of operating. You need to be aware of your preference when making a career choice. For example, an introvert might do well in research, but would do very poorly as a salesperson. An extrovert, who was highly successful at leading a fundraising campaign, making speeches, and meeting people, would likely be very unhappy spending the day in an office analyzing data.

Herbert Sanders, operations manager for a manufacturing company in the Northeast, had this to say: "A candidate can have lots of skills and experience, but if he or she doesn't enjoy the work or fit in with the rest of the team, it's a lost cause. I hire only those who meet all three of the qualifications—skills, desire, and fit. These ingredients have to be a good mix in order for people to be successful in my department."

Sanders is not alone in his thinking. Be sure the job is right for you in all three categories. To accept anything less could be disastrous.

As you search for a new occupation or career goal, keep in mind that you'll want to consider a variety of things before making a change. It's important to base your decision on interests, values, skills, and personality traits. Avoid selecting a new career based on only one or two criteria.

Myth #7

Resumes get jobs.

Reality

A resume opens the door. The interview gets the job.

Discussion

The interview provides 99 percent of the necessary information to those considering you. The interview is where employers make hiring decisions. So you may wonder, "Why spend time on a resume if it's not that important?"

The resume serves as a "letter of introduction." It did its job if you successfully passed the prospective employer's initial review. It might help to think about the resume from the viewpoint of the reader.

Different resume readers approach resumes from different angles. Some readers will compare your resume to others they've received. Others approach it as a critical deciding factor as to whether or not your qualifications meet the requirements of the job; they have no interest in someone who "almost" matches that criteria. Then you have people who don't hesitate to judge a resume based on their personal biases; they often have criteria that only they understand. Larger companies frequently have someone in the human resources department who screens resumes before sending them to hiring managers for further review.

Faced with all of the above, your job is to prepare a resume that highlights your experience and potential without including unnecessary details that might confuse the reader.

Resumes can screen you in or out. To improve your chances for being screened in, consider these guidelines:

- Is your resume brief (two pages or less) and to the point? Employers don't need (or want) your life history, only an overview of what you have to offer.
- Is it free of spelling and grammatical errors? Mistakes can eliminate you from consideration; they suggest you don't pay attention to detail.
- Is it obvious that you have transferable skills that you could use in any industry?
- Is your resume uncrowded, or does it look congested? You don't want to present a resume that's visually intimidating.
- Have you clearly communicated what you have to offer an employer?
- Have you avoided technical language that might confuse the reader? Keep in mind that in most cases, two people will screen your resume: a human resources professional and then the decision-maker.

After you finish your resume, you should know what's on it. That may sound obvious, but many people fail to take this important step. When someone asks you questions about your experience or credentials, you need to be able to supply the same information that's on your resume without hesitation.

In addition to the above, keep in mind two more questions:

- Can you support with evidence the training, skills, and work experiences you've listed on your resume?
- Can you prove you can do what you claim you have done?

Trying to improve your resume by overstating your qualifications could lead to an embarrassing situation later in the interview process.

Example: Kenneth Wilkins, an energetic and ambitious man, was interested in a job in his field (building maintenance), but realized the position required more schooling and experience than he could offer. So he decided to do some "minor work" on his resume because he "almost" had the necessary qualifications. At first reading, the resume looked fine; he even got a phone call for an interview. Then things began to unravel. The half-truths and embellishments surfaced and the job possibility quickly evaporated. To make matters worse, others in the industry heard about what he had tried to do and the incident tarnished his reputation. He had prepared a resume that opened the door, but it quickly slammed shut during the interview process once the truth was discovered.

Let a well-written, honest resume open the door for you. When you get to the interview, sell yourself by convincing the interviewer that you have both the aptitude and the attitude the company is seeking.

Myth #8

Resumes should always include a job objective.

Reality

The reality is two-fold:

1. When an objective on a "generic" resume is too specific, you can lose opportunities.
2. When an objective is too broad, you'd be better off without one.

Discussion

If you're looking for a specific type of job, and are limited to that job alone, then use a specific objective.

For example, you're seeking a position as a controller and that's the only opportunity you're willing to accept. Your resume could read:

       Job Objective: Controller

If you have multiple career interests in the same field, your objective could read:

       Job Objective: Controller/Assistant Controller/VP–Finance

The difference may be the type of organization to which you're applying for a job. A controller position in a medium-size company may be perfect for you; but in a large company you would qualify best for an assistant controller job. In a small company, a vice president of finance position may be ideal.

If you decide to include more than one objective, each should be in a related field at a similar level of responsibility.

Examples: Taylor Gibbs qualified as a secretary, an administrative assistant, and an executive assistant. Her resume reflected all three. Gibbs' job search led to several offers, including the one she accepted as an administrative assistant in a high school guidance department.

Bill Wyatt sought a position as a recreational therapist. He also qualified as an occupational therapist. In addition, he had experience with seniors as well as children. His job objective encompassed all of these. He accepted a job as an occupational therapist in a center for developmentally disabled adults and children.

Candy Clarke studied television broadcasting in college. Her goal was to become a sports commentator. "I've been a sports nut since I was a kid. My uncle worked for NBC Sports and I loved spending time with him on the job. However, when I finished school, the labor market was tight and I found I had to adjust my goals. I ended up using several different job objectives on my resume based on the kind of job the employer had available. After a lot of interviews, I accepted a job in the public relations department of a brewery that sponsored sporting events as part of its public relations program. I love what I do, but it took getting creative with my job objectives to get noticed."

A broad job objective that is really more of a career objective, such as "seeking a challenging career with a growth-oriented organization that will allow for creativity and autonomy," takes up valuable space on a resume and offers little information. Include a more specific job objective instead, or leave it off the resume. You could also tailor your cover letter to accomplish the same thing that a job objective would offer on a resume.

Caution: Don't simply change the title or wording of the career or job objective without making changes to the resume itself. In order to be effective, your resume should reflect your qualifications and ability for the specific career objective you list.

Myth #9

It's important to include on your resume every job you've ever held.

Reality

Too much information provides the reader with little incentive to meet you in person.

Discussion

The purpose of the resume is to generate enough interest so that you'll be invited for an interview. Don't overwhelm the reader with prior work experience that may not be related to your current job search. Include only the last 10 years of previous work history.

For more senior candidates who've held several positions, or have worked with the same employer for many years, it's not necessary to go back 25 years with work history on a resume. Just include a statement that says, for example, "Work experience prior to (year) included positions as a controller, budget analyst, and cost accounting clerk." This tells the reader you've held several other positions and progressed in responsibility. If the interviewers want more information, they'll ask.

Include mention of other work experience if you think it's related to the job for which you're applying. For example: a candidate applying for a retail sales position may want to mention clerking in a department store during the summers to pay for college tuition. In this instance, an employer interested in hiring a sales manager or store assistant would probably find someone with even short-term work experience in the retail industry attractive.

In another situation, candidates applying for entry-level management positions who've managed people, even if 15 years ago, may have an advantage over candidates who have no prior managerial experience. There are some things you don't forget and employers will recognize the value of (even if not recent) managerial experience.

If this is your first job after high school or college and you don't have any full-time work experience, include part-time and temporary work. Cooperative education experience can give you a head start too. You can also list volunteer work, especially if it's applicable to your career field.

Example: Wanda Stone started with a seven-page resume. She included information about previous jobs for the past 26 years. She listed references as well as hobbies and interests. She had no idea that her resume was annoying employers. She met a career counselor who critiqued her resume and told her to reduce it to two pages, which she did. From then on, she was more attractive in the eyes of prospective employers. Soon thereafter, she found a job she enjoys.

Concentrate on what you have to offer. Show employers that you've taken the initiative to get a job, regardless of what it was. Everyone has to start somewhere; employers know that.

Bob Tanner, a human resource manager, had this to add: "I like to see resumes that are short, well-written, and give me a good sense of what the candidate has done in previous jobs. A resume longer than two pages is often filled with unnecessary fluff. Candidates have the best chance of getting an interview with me if they stick to the facts and keep it brief."

Myth #10

It's a good idea to include a photograph with your resume.

Reality

Employers are more likely to eliminate you from consideration if you include a photograph.

Discussion

Improve your chances for making the first cut by including only those things about yourself that are job-related, factual, and likely to get you an invitation to an interview with a decision-maker.

Maybe you think that a picture of you looking your best will help you get an interview. But consider the following possible reactions: You may remind the interviewer of the creep who sat behind her in sixth grade. She hated him because he kept kicking her chair during tests in an effort to break her concentration. Maybe your slightly crooked smile, which you always thought was cute, reminds the recruiter of the girl who at the last minute stood him up for the junior prom. You may "appear" too heavy, too thin, too serious, too excitable, too light or too dark, or even too sexy.

Examples: Sally Kerner believed that a glamorous photograph would help her get an interview. She didn't get a call, however, and it was several months later before she found out why. She knew someone who worked in the human resources department of the company to which she had applied, and that person finally told her how the company reacted upon seeing the picture. The sexy photograph had quickly eliminated Kerner from further consideration.

When Troy Maysick submitted a photograph, he encountered the same results but for a different reason. He was considerably overweight and had a "five o'clock shadow" in the photograph. He looked like someone who was sloppy and neglectful of his appearance. Prospective employers weren't interested in him because he seemed to be a misfit for the job.

In reality, both candidates had the qualifications for the jobs but lost the opportunities because of a photograph.

Keep them guessing until they meet you. Let them base their preliminary judgment on your skills, work experience, and educational qualifications. As is commonly said, "A picture's worth a thousand words." However, while job hunting it belongs at home, in a frame, on the mantel, above the fireplace.

On another note, employers cannot require you to submit a photograph or ask you to agree to be photographed for a company identification badge or other reasons until *after* you're hired. (This and other inappropriate pre-employment requests are covered in Appendix D.)

Myth #11

Functional resumes aren't as effective as chronological resumes.

Reality

An effective resume, whether in a functional or chronological style, is one that arouses the curiosity of the reader.

Discussion

The chronological format is used most frequently. It lists work experience in reverse-time sequence with an emphasis on responsibilities, skills, accomplishments, and academic or professional distinctions.

The functional resume format emphasizes your skills rather than listing specific jobs held in sequential order.

To decide which format is best for you, consider the following:

The chronological resume is effective when:
- Your work history shows progress.
- You want to emphasize marketable, transferable skills.
- You've worked for well-known employers.

- You're applying for a job in a traditional field such as nursing, engineering, law, finance, education, or with the government.

The functional resume is effective when:
- You're changing careers.
- You've had several jobs in a short period of time.
- You've been demoted in job responsibility.
- You've been unemployed for 1 year or more.

You may also decide to *combine chronological and functional elements into the same resume.* This technique can help you if you want to:

- Emphasize your unique skills and accomplishments.
- De-emphasize certain parts of your employment history.

This format may be particularly useful for midlife and older workers. If you're unsure which style to use, prepare a resume in all three formats. Then compare them and see which style presents you in the best possible light to a prospective employer. You may also want to ask several other people to compare them and give you an opinion.

Whether you use the functional or chronological style or a combination of the two, be sure your resume is visually attractive (has enough white space), interesting, concise, and contains facts and details that prove your value as an employee. As always, it must be free of grammatical, spelling, and typographical errors.

Sandra Owens, a general manager for a restaurant chain, had this to say: "I see hundreds of resumes every year. They're written in different styles; some don't seem to follow any particular format. The bottom line is that I need to be able to quickly scan them to determine whether or not the applicants meet my needs. I don't care if it's functional or chronological. In fact, I've always used a functional format in preparing my own resume as I feel I'm better able to market my experience that way."

Myth #12

The more information you have on your resume, the better.

Reality

Less can be more.

Discussion

Keep your resume to one page, two pages at most. If you need two pages, the second page should be at least three-fourths full. Readers tend to disregard pages with small amounts of information. If your resume runs more than two pages, you need to edit it for brevity, clarity, and content.

If you still don't believe three pages is too much, ask a friend to read your resume. Watch closely, and you'll notice that by the time he or she gets to page three they're probably reading faster and faster just trying to finish.

Although the structure of a resume will vary according to which format you choose (see Myth #11), the following is a general outline for a standard resume:

- *Name, address, and telephone number* including area code at the top of your resume.

- *Job objective*, if you choose to use one (see Myth #8).
- *Employment record*, beginning with your present or most recent position (see Myth #9). After the company name, dates of employment, and job title, include a statement that explains how your experience at that company was valuable. Some people prefer to divide their employment experience into two groups: the experience that pertains directly to the job for which they're applying, and experience that does not.
- *Education.* List your GPA if it's high (3.5 or above on a 4.0 scale), otherwise leave it off the resume. It's not necessary to mention your high school education if you have a college degree. If you don't have a college degree, then you'll want to list schools and relevant courses taken. The education section can be particularly important if you have only limited employment experience. Highlight ways you can use your education in the job for which you're applying.
- *Special information.* Don't list everything you've ever done here, but mention something that may have impact on your suitability for the position (e.g., a second language, awards earned, honors bestowed, certification completed such as a CPA, etc.)

Instead of using excess verbiage to prove your point, tailor your resume to show how past accomplishments meet the specific employer's criteria. Consider the following:

- Use a brief summary of accomplishments rather than an objective statement that can make you appear limited in qualifications.
- Lead with experience, not education. Employers are more interested in your work experience than your education, so include education at the end.
- Detail your job history by writing accomplishment statements, not just job duties. (See Appendix A for samples.)
- List relevant activities, but not so many as to overwhelm the reader. Use only those activities that relate directly to your self-improvement efforts and the position you're seeking.
- Don't put negative information on your resume (e.g., that you prefer not to travel or are not interested in relocating). You may have a legitimate reason for these things, and with the proper explanation during an interview it may not be a problem. However, if you put the information on the resume (e.g., "Prefer limited travel"), you may

eliminate yourself from consideration, even if the job doesn't require travel, because it sounds negative to the reader.

In summary, include only information that is necessary to attract the attention of the interviewer. Too much detail provides little reason for someone to contact you for a personal interview. Too much information may also provide the interviewer with information that he or she interprets negatively and that you may never have the opportunity to defend.

A well-written, concise resume can be "more" in the eyes of the reader.

Myth #13

Including your age, race, marital status, height, weight, and religion on your resume gives it a personal touch.

Reality

A potential employer's knowledge of personal information could result in discrimination against you.

Discussion

Include only the information that's necessary to get an interview (see Myth #12).

- Name, address, and telephone number.
- Job objective.
- Employment experience.
- Education.
- Honors/awards/special achievements.

You don't need to list reasons for having left a job, former or desired salary, hobbies, or the words "References will be furnished upon request." It's none of their business (at least at this point in the job search process) why you left a previous employer. If they know your past salary history or current requirements, they may decide to eliminate you before you have a chance to sell yourself and convince them you're worth the money you want. It's taken for granted that you will provide references if asked. Height, weight, religion, marital status, race, and age are no one's business but yours.

When you supply personal information on a resume, you're making available information to which hiring managers are not entitled. Someone may form any number of biased opinions based on that information. Examples: They may assume that you'll have a heavy accent (nationality), that you'll have an absenteeism problem (young children), that you'll have health problems (weight), etc. Once you're in an interview situation, however, you have the opportunity to sell yourself as a candidate and overcome any such biases.

Bob Mathis, a human resources manager for a multi-billion-dollar retailer, had this to say about what to include and what not to include on a resume: "I see literally thousands of resumes every year. Candidates who include personal information lose valuable space that should be devoted to selling major accomplishments. Of course, there's the additional issue of putting yourself at risk and out of consideration for a job because of something that's on a resume. I don't even recommend listing social, fraternal, or civic involvement because it could be construed as negative. Stick to the facts. Do the rest when you're invited for a personal interview."

Although discrimination is against the law, it does exist. Don't make it easy for someone to use your personal information to take you out of the selection process because of his or her personal bias.

Myth #14

It's a good strategy to list references on your resume.

Reality

Don't give prospective employers the chance to check references and possibly eliminate you from consideration before you've been interviewed.

Discussion

References can be a critical deciding factor as to whether someone hires you. Be prepared to provide, *when requested,* a list of references who will speak highly of you as an individual and as a former employee. And make sure these people know you've listed them as a reference. The following job seekers provide two examples of what *not* to do.

Examples: Albert Santiago included his references at the bottom of his resume. The prospective employer called the references before contacting Santiago for an interview. The employer became concerned about a statement one reference made about his reliability. In reality, the reference had him confused with someone else. The reference cost Santiago an interview which may have led to a job offer.

41

Becky Marist didn't have a list of references ready when asked, so she faxed them to the interviewer. The list contained one reference fewer than had been requested and two of the people listed were personal friends. The interviewer began to contact the references. The first reference was not aware that she had given his name and was unprepared for the interviewer's call. One number was disconnected and another was always busy. Though qualified for the job, Marist's references may have lost her a potential job opportunity.

When an interviewer asks for your references, it's a sign that a job offer is likely to follow or at least that you're among the finalists. Always have three to five *work-related references* typed on a separate sheet of paper and ready to give to the interviewer.

Information about each reference should include:

- Name.
- Job title.
- Relationship to you (e.g., previous supervisor, former high school English teacher, co-worker, or others who know you).
- Address including zip code.
- Telephone number including area code.
- Fax number and e-mail address, if available.

Notify the references that someone may contact them. Job offers sometimes don't materialize because a reference is surprised by a call regarding a former employee. The prospective employer knows immediately that you didn't notify in advance the people you used as references.

Most employers want to speak with people for whom you've worked. Former supervisors are best. Use a co-worker only if you are short one reference. Also, be sure each person you list understands the importance of serving as a reference. Neutral references, ones that aren't convincing, can cost you a job offer.

Remember these two points:

1. Never give prospective employers more information on your resume than they need to know. If they want more, they'll ask for it.
2. Never go to a job interview without your list of work-related references who are ready to convince prospective employers that you're the best person for the job.

(See Myths #54 and #55 for additional information on references.)

Myth #15

Plain resumes don't get fancy job offers.

Reality

Skip the fluff and write a promotional advertising piece that gets the reader's attention. That's how you win invitations for interviews that lead to fancy job offers.

Discussion

The word "fancy" means different things to different people. However, employers are looking for the facts as they quickly scan your resume. They don't care about interesting fonts, scented paper, or exaggerated graphics. Stick with a simple, clean layout that emphasizes what you can do for them. Your goal when creating a resume is to describe your skills accurately and persuasively (see Myth #7).

If you believe it is weak you might feel tempted to "fill out" your resume with additional wording that sounds good but may not really say anything important. You know you have past accomplishments to list, but suddenly your brain seems to have forgotten all of them. Maybe you've been at the same job so long it's difficult to recall past successes. You may need to do some research to help produce your best resume.

Good resource materials for preparing your resume include: old resumes, samples of your work (reports, projects, newsletters, etc.), old date books, newspaper or magazine clippings about your accomplishments, performance evaluations, etc. These items can help prod your memory, especially if it's been awhile since you've prepared a resume.

Follow these simple resume guidelines:

- Consolidate similar accomplishments. Make sure they fit the job you're seeking. List the most important accomplishments first.
- If you have an interest in several types of jobs, prepare a separate resume for each type. Customize them and use the "buzz" words of the industry to attract attention.
- Create a skills summary that shows your accomplishments in chronological order.
- If you don't have a lot of work experience, include part-time or summer jobs, unpaid internships, and volunteer work. Your resume doesn't have to look barren nor do you have to fabricate information just because you're new to the job market.

"Fancy" job offers depend on:

- Developing a resume that gets the initial interview.
- Convincing the decision-maker you have the "right stuff" to do the job.
- Appearing to be a good "fit" with the rest of the employees.
- Knowing what you're worth in the job market.
- Aiming for what you're worth in terms of compensation.
- Understanding the basic principles of effective salary negotiations.

Don't overload your resume with filler material and lofty, long-term goals. If you want the employer's attention, make sure the resume has adequate white space and is visually appealing in its simplicity of format.

Myth #16

Mass mailing resumes is an effective job-search strategy.

Reality

Mass mailing is like throwing resumes into the trash. It's a waste of time and money.

Discussion

It's a mystery how this myth started. However, today too many job seekers aim at every target, whether or not there's a job fit. Companies are bombarded with resumes, query letters, phone calls, and walk-in traffic.

There's a better way to reach large numbers of prospective employers who are more apt to be interested. That effective strategy is called *targeted mailing*. The difference is that you carefully identify organizations for which you believe you'd be a good match. In addition to known job openings, research companies that have recruited people like you in the past. Even though they may not be hiring at the moment, there's a good likelihood they'll need someone with your qualifications again.

Here's how the different approaches worked for two job seekers.

Example: Alice and Jeannie Dalton of San Francisco are identical twins who decided to experiment with two different approaches to the job market. Both women sought work in brand management. Jeannie mass mailed 500 cover letters with resumes. Alice carefully targeted companies with which she had something in common. Jeannie received replies from 2 percent of those she contacted. Alice got responses from 15 percent and four job offers followed. It took Jeannie 6 months to find an acceptable position, whereas Alice was working within 3 months.

As you prepare to contact businesses by mail, consider the following:

- Identify organizations that are of interest to you and that you believe have the most potential for hiring you. Consider type of work, salary requirements, your geographical preferences, and reputation of the company in the industry.
- Research to learn more about them. Dun & Bradstreet, as well as state, county, or city company directories, can provide you with this information. Check your local library.
- Develop a marketing letter that is no more than two pages in length to serve as a cover letter for your resume. The letter should briefly describe your accomplishments and how you may fit into their organization. Don't include personal information such as age, marital status, race, or salary history. The employer could use this information to discriminate against you.
- At the end of the letter, include a "thank you" for their time in reading your resume.
- Follow up with a telephone call. Try to get an appointment for a personal interview. Be persistent. Many job seekers give up too easily.

Targeted mailing takes time and requires you to do your homework. Mass mailing may seem easier initially, but in the long run doesn't pay off as well. In addition to a low response rate, the responses you receive may not be fruitful—particularly if you mass mailed blindly without carefully considering the recipients of your letters. You may receive an invitation to interview and then realize belatedly that you have absolutely no interest in working for that company.

Although, as I'll discuss in Myth #39, every interview is a rehearsal for the one that brings the job offer and is also a chance to get your foot in the door, you don't want to spend excessive amounts of time interviewing for the wrong jobs.

Myth #17

The best way to send a resume is by mail or fax.

Reality

Electronic resumes offer special advantages over those sent by mail or fax.

Discussion

Although networking and other traditional methods of job hunting are effective, the electronic age offers alternatives for making business contacts. As Intel's Web page explains: the resumes they receive "are scanned into a database using optical character recognition technology." Intel recruiters perform regular searches of the database to find qualified candidates for open jobs. Searches are done by key words and phrases that describe skills and core course work required for each job. It's important that resumes include terms and familiar industry acronyms for all relevant skills.

Electronic Resume Revolution, Joyce Lain Kennedy's book co-authored with Thomas Morrow, recommends mimicking a job advertisement in order to feed back the key words that the employer used to describe the job. This will ensure that your resume is located during a database search.

Brenda Sax, a vice president with an international outplacement firm, sees the Web as a powerful tool for job seekers: "It's a great way to network and research companies and industries. In addition, scanning resumes makes my job easier and helps job hunters get their information out immediately to hundreds of prospective employers."

Forms for resume writing are also available on the Web. They vary from simple to complex. *Resumix* offers one continuous form. When finished the job seeker hits a button and has an instantly formatted resume. *Intellimatch* walks the job seeker through a series of categories to write a detailed resume.

For information on how to organize your resume, start by reading advice on the Web such as *Job Smart* (type in "Job Smart"). For design advice, try *The Riley Guide* by Margaret Riley (dbm.com/jobguide).

A free public resume database called *ResumeCM* (www.careermosaic. com) hosts 55,000+ resumes. It's free to anyone who wants to post a resume. You fill out an on-line form with information such as your name, address, telephone number, e-mail address, and current job title. Then you "paste" your resume in the space provided. It will appear exactly as you've entered it, which means lines with more than 65 characters may run off the screen. There's a preview feature that allows you to see how your resume will appear.

Hundreds of on-line resume databases are available today. You'll want to find out what each database offers and decide which one suits your needs best.

If you're a college student seeking full-time employment upon graduation consider the following college recruitment sites:

- www.bridgepath.com
- www.careermag.com
- www.collegegrad.com
- www.hotwired.com
- www.jobdirect.com
- www.jobhunt.com
- www.jobtrak.com
- www.jobweb.org
- www.purdue.edu
- www.rpi.edu

One word of caution: Once you put your resume on-line, it's available to anyone who wants to read it. If you don't want your present employer or business associates to know you're looking for something else, you may decide the Internet is not the place to conduct a job search.

There's one more set of guidelines to consider when preparing your resume; that's creating a resume that's scannable. Although not every company today uses a database to store resumes, the practice is becoming more popular.

The computer will look for standard resume sections. If you've used headings or divisions that aren't standard, your resume may be overlooked when the employer searches the database for possible candidates for a job.

People involved in the hiring process use key words or certain criteria when they use the database to search for resumes for job openings. They may also look for skills inventories that match the job needs. Your resume will need to contain those key words to attract attention.

Follow these simple guidelines to help make your resume scannable:

- Use a standard resume format for headings.
- Use simple typefaces, with font size of 10 to 14 points.
- Use bold or all capital letters for headings.
- Avoid underlining, italics, graphics, lines on the page, etc.
- Print your name at the top of each page on a line by itself.
- Print your address below your name.
- Print phone numbers on separate lines.
- Use light-colored paper that has a smooth surface (white, off-white, light cream).
- Use a laser printer if possible, or photocopies of high quality.
- Don't fold your letter and resume; mail in a large envelope.

If you have a resume and cover letter that are in step with the latest technology, you've got a head start on applicants whose resumes aren't compatible with a database system. (See Appendix B for an Internet Glossary.)

Myth #18

It's acceptable not to use a cover letter with your resume.

Reality

Use a cover letter with every resume unless the ad explicitly states that the applicant should not include one.

Discussion

Your cover letter is your calling card. If they like your cover letter, they're likely to read your resume.

Writing cover letters can be difficult. It takes practice to explain how your credentials are of benefit to prospective employers. Remember these two main points about your cover letter:

1. *Keep it simple, to the point, and free of clutter.* Like a resume, there should be enough white space to make it attractive to the reader's eye.
2. *Customize it.* Generic cover letters won't convince the reader that you're a match. Highlight the aspects of your background that will attract attention.

Write the letter in three parts:

1. The *introduction* is the first paragraph. State why you're writing. If you're responding to an ad, state which job you're applying for and where you saw it advertised. If someone referred you, mention his or her name. Indicate some knowledge of the organization and the reason for your interest in working there.
2. The *body* of the cover letter should describe your qualifications for the job. Highlight your education and the achievements that qualify you. (Be sure to research the company and the position so you'll know what sells.) This is your chance to tell a prospective employer why you're the best person for the position.
3. The *close* or final paragraph should re-emphasize your interest and what you want to happen next. You may indicate that you'll call the employer to arrange a convenient meeting time. An alternative is to express a desire to meet with the employer and request that he or she call you to schedule an interview. Finally, say thank you for their time and consideration in reading your letter.

The following basics should be adhered to as you write your cover letter:

-   Use personalized letterhead stationary. You can create it on your computer.
-   Address the letter to a specific person by both name and title. Make as many phone calls as needed to get this information. This will help you avoid salutations such as, "Dear Sir," "Dear Madam," or "To Whom it May Concern," which are too impersonal and may annoy the reader.
-   Group similar thoughts together, then organize the paragraphs in logical order, using the above guidelines.
-   Hold the reader's attention by varying sentence structure and length.
-   Focus on three or four of your strongest qualities and tie them to the qualifications needed for the job. Use bullets to draw the reader's attention to these items.
-   Be positive in content, tone, and word choice.
-   Avoid technical jargon, especially if you think the reader may not understand.
-   Don't be redundant. Cover letters should include additional/different information, not be just another version of your resume.

- Keep it to one page if possible, and certainly no more than two. Your goal is to get them interested enough to read your resume.
- Be sure it's free from spelling and grammatical errors. Ask a friend or family member to check it and re-check it.

If you're making a career change, your cover letter may allow you to get your foot in the door with a skeptical hiring manager. It provides the opportunity to persuade him or her to interview you in spite of your apparent lack of experience in the field. You will, of course, have researched the company to which you're applying. Then, in your cover letter you can state that you realize you aren't a perfect match based on the job description, but that you believe your education and experience, plus your enthusiasm, will more than compensate for your non-traditional profile.

For some final advice Ed Scranton, a recruiter and former human resources executive, had this to say: "Every resume must have a cover letter, but it should be more than just fluff. The primary purpose of the cover letter is to provide a brief and accurate account of your qualifications—no more—no less. I don't bother to read resumes that don't have cover letters. It tells me the candidate didn't prepare for one of the first steps in the job search process, writing a cover letter to go with the resume. It's not difficult to write. Just do it."

Myth #19

A handwritten cover letter conveys a feeling of warmth.

Reality

A handwritten cover letter shows a lack of professionalism.

Discussion

Apart from the fact that the business world considers a handwritten cover letter tacky, there are many other reasons why it makes sense not to use one. Some people have almost unintelligible handwriting. If someone can't read what you've written, it's hard for your qualifications to impress him or her. Some people's handwriting looks sloppy. Maybe your handwriting appears rather immature and childish in style. Sometimes ink smears. The lines of handwritten letters often have a tendency to slope up or down on the page. A handwritten cover letter looks, and is, unprofessional.

Prepare your cover letter as carefully as you prepare your resume. In addition to the items mentioned in Myth #18, remember two important points:

1. Prepare the letter on the same type of paper you use for your resume;
2. Use a laser-quality printer. Anything less is unacceptable if you want to be competitive.

Tim Blaylock summed it up: "As a recruiter and business owner, I've seen all kinds of cover letters. I throw away those that are handwritten. I've found over the years that candidates who don't know enough to type a cover letter have resumes that aren't worth reading. If those same candidates get as far as the interview, they're usually not prepared and waste my time."

Example: Betsy Glade is an example of someone who ignored the rules and wasn't allowed to play the game. "I have worked since I was 16 years old. I'm 42 now. I not only hand-wrote cover letters, but sometimes resumes if I didn't have access to a typewriter or computer. I have a pretty tough attitude in that I believe that what they see is what they get. If they don't like my informal style, they won't like me either."

Glade's attitude and unwillingness to be competitive in the way she presented herself through her cover letter and resume cost her numerous interview opportunities. Although she eventually networked her way into a job she enjoys, it took her much longer to find it than necessary.

Whether you're responding to an advertisement in the newspaper, a job posting, or a position you've become aware of through a friend, your cover letter is just as important as your resume.

Myth #20

Generic, mass-produced cover letters are effective for certain positions.

Reality

A generic, mass-produced cover letter shows insincerity and therefore is not likely to get the attention you want. Whether you offer highly specialized technical skills, or experience that's easy to get, your approach to preparing a cover letter is the same: tailor your letter for each job.

Discussion

Communication skills are among the most important skills you bring to a job. Every cover letter you write carries a message about you and your ability to communicate.

Consider the following as you promote your candidacy through cover letters:

- Design your cover letter to be work-centered and employer-centered, not self-centered. Your letter should address the needs of the specific employer and evoke a desire to learn more about you.

- Tailor your letter for each job and stress the benefits of hiring you.
- Sign the letter in a different color ink than the one used to print the letter. This emphasizes the individuality of the letter, as opposed to a cover letter with a photocopied signature.

Example: Patrick Hodges decided to save time and effort by making copies of his cover letter at the local office supply store. Although some of the copies appeared fairly neat, others were slightly off center on the page, a couple of them had spots, and the paper wasn't high-grade bond. The information in the letter was very general because he was sending it to a variety of prospective employers. Although he signed each letter individually, the fact that it was a generic, mass-produced letter was obvious to the reader.

Hodges had an excellent resume, well-prepared and printed on good quality paper. Unfortunately his cover letter "sank" the resume in two ways. First, it didn't have enough information to entice the reader to look at the resume. Second, those who did continue to read the resume wondered why someone who had obviously taken time to prepare a good resume would use such an inadequate cover letter. This gave the reader the impression that Hodges didn't care enough to take care of the details and finish the job right.

A generic, mass-produced cover letter tells employers that you didn't consider their jobs important enough to spend time preparing an individualized letter or that you didn't know any better.

Myth #21

Unusual-looking cover letters and resumes make you stand out.

Reality

You want them to remember you for your job qualifications, not your unconventional resume. Stick to the standard professional look.

Discussion

Job seekers who use pink, blue, green, or red paper (or any other non-neutral color) for cover letters and resumes don't usually succeed in getting interviews. Why? Because they look odd compared to the more conservative white or off-white paper used by the competition. Unusually thick or over-sized paper is also inappropriate.

Example: Tonya Hinkleman summed it up this way: "I thought since I didn't have much work experience, I'd get attention by using pale lavender paper for my resume. It was almost as thick as construction paper. My two-page resume required two stamps. I was proud of it, but was embarrassed when a recruiter told me it was the reason I wasn't getting called for interviews. I thought he was crazy and continued to print and send it on thick, lavender paper. I eventually got smarter and figured out what the recruiter said was the truth. Unfortunately, I was passed up by companies who must have thought I was a radical."

Hinkleman finally got the job she wanted, and 10 years later became a career counselor in a college career services office. She often shares her "lavender paper" story with her students, who get a good laugh from her mistake.

Note: On rare occasions, a very clever and unusual cover letter will attract the recruiter's attention. However, it's best to stay with the "tried and true." You're taking a big chance otherwise. Unless they're specifically looking for a "non-conformist," recruiters and interviewers won't look favorably upon glitzy or strange cover letters and resumes.

THE CAMPAIGN

Conducting a job search, whether you're employed or unemployed, is a challenge. You'll need a good attitude and stamina to survive. Stay in shape, or get in shape. Keep up your spirits. Physical and mental health are important to your success in finding a job that's right for you. Good health also contributes to your self-confidence. Candidates who have a high level of self-confidence favorably impress prospective employers and networking contacts.

In addition to feeling good, you'll want to keep yourself organized. Establish a system for maintaining accurate records of networking contacts and calls. It's easy to confuse discussions and information as you collect more data with each passing day.

If you're hesitant about networking, keep in mind that networking isn't about using people; it's about making connections to job opportunities through social and business contacts. Also, remember that you're not asking your network contacts for a job. You're seeking advice about industries and opportunities.

When networking, be sure you have a clear strategy in mind and an objective for the discussion or you'll be seen as a time-waster. Respect their time; they have jobs to do too. Meet with them at their convenience and thank them for their assistance. If you leave a message and don't get a response, don't pester the contact. You need to be persistent, but you also need to know when to take a hint that there's no interest in helping you.

Since individuals and companies today use voice mail systems for messages, you will likely encounter them when making telephone calls. If you decide to leave a message, keep it brief. Pronounce your name clearly. Mention the name of the person who suggested you call (or whatever connection you have to the person you're calling). Leave your phone number and say you'll call back. After you've left three messages with no response, send a letter instead of calling again.

In addition, be discreet in giving out business cards. Wait for the right time and place and never make a big deal out of it.

The myths/realities in Part II can help you avoid some of the most common mistakes job seekers make. It also provides practical suggestions for starting and maintaining your job search over an extended period of time.

Part II includes the following myths:

22. Any job is better than no job.
23. Interim or temporary jobs seldom lead to permanent positions.
24. It's okay to use the informational interview to ask about a job.
25. The best way to find a job is to broadcast to the largest number of people possible.
26. Most job openings appear in newspaper advertisements.
27. The Human Resources Department is the best place to start your job search.
28. Job fairs seldom lead to job offers.
29. It's difficult using the Internet to conduct a job search.
30. Networking is sleazy.
31. Long-distance job hunting is a waste of time.
32. The best jobs are in high-growth industries.
33. Companies don't hire during the December holidays.
34. If companies aren't hiring, there's nothing you can do about it.
35. Researching a company isn't as important as how you present your skills and abilities in a personal interview.
36. Recruiters are in business to find employment for job seekers.
37. When questioning recruiters about job openings, you run the risk of alienating them.
38. All employment agencies are alike.

Myth #22

Any job is better than no job.

Reality

If you hastily accept whatever comes along because it's easier than looking for the right opportunity, you may find yourself in an uncomfortable situation.

Discussion

This myth seems logical. After all, you need money to live. However, consider the following case.

Example: Rick Kryzinski, a recent college graduate, took a position that didn't particularly interest him because it was the only job offer he got. Rather than put additional effort into his search, he took the easy way out. He lasted 7 months. They fired him because he was frequently late for work, conducted personal business on company time, and had been caught playing games on his computer when he should have been working. He tried to defend himself, but his supervisor didn't buy his story.

Although he didn't want to admit the job loss upset him, being terminated from his first job left him with low self-esteem. He also had to restart his job search with an unfavorable reference from his former employer. Taking a short cut created a dilemma that Kryzinski spent months resolving.

Consider the following as you evaluate job offers:

- How well do you think you'll fit with the company's culture?
- Is there enough challenge?
- Is there room for advancement?
- Will the company provide training? If so, how much and what kind?
- What does your family think about the job opportunity?
- Will you have to relocate? How do you feel about that?
- If the position involves travel, is it too much or just right?
- How many hours per week will they expect you to work?
- What's the company's reputation in the industry?
- When is the last time they had a lay-off?
- Are the pay and benefits sufficient to support your lifestyle?

These questions must be asked and answered truthfully before accepting a job offer. Maybe sitting at a desk all day isn't enough to keep you interested. You may find more success in a sales environment where you'll have a lot of contact with people. You may regret your decision if you didn't weigh these questions seriously.

Once you've answered the previous questions, ask yourself one more thing:

> Do I view this opportunity as a suitable career position or just a job to help me get what I need for now?

Example: Pete Kelley, a successful businessman, had this to say about his search for a new position: "I accepted a job in banking when what I really wanted was something with a brokerage firm. Rather than put more energy into my search, I accepted the first offer I got. I was unhappy from the start and my employer knew it. Finally, we mutually agreed that it was best that I leave."

If you have to have work, it's okay if you decide to accept what you can get rather than keep looking for the right or better opportunity. But it's not okay if you're accepting "any old job that comes along" because it's easier than working hard to find the right position.

Some job seekers look for the path of least resistance, then complain that they hate the job they have. Don't let that happen to you.

In short, know what you want. Define your criteria. Focus on finding employment that meets your needs. Don't be willing to accept a poor fit just because it's easier than continuing to search. Sometimes, no job is better than a bad choice.

Myth #23

Interim or temporary jobs seldom lead to permanent positions.

Reality

Interesting opportunities as a temporary professional can and often do lead to permanent positions.

Discussion

Many people have improved their chances for getting a permanent position by working as a long-term temporary employee. Jay Marnie provides an excellent example. He found a permanent position in the broadcast industry through a long-term temporary assignment.

"After losing my job due to downsizing," said Marnie, "I decided a temporary job would add variety to my career. It provided income and bridged the gap between employers. It also did a lot for my self-esteem."

However, interim jobs, like permanent positions, should fit your overall career strategy. For example, accepting an assignment as a supervisor in a manufacturing environment would be a mistake if that's not the direction you want your career to take and you have no interest in exploring that field.

Think of a temporary job as an opportunity to:

- Gain practical work experience.
- Develop or enhance your skills.
- Explore a career field.
- Meet people who may know where there's a job for you.
- Bridge the gap between where you are and where you want to be.
- Earn income to support yourself during the interim.

Most, though not all temporary jobs come through agencies, which means you'll need to register with agencies that handle the type of work in which you're interested. If you're looking to change careers, you may want to register with a temporary agency that advertises for multi-disciplinary skills. Networking is also an excellent way to learn about temporary professional jobs.

Whether you're seeking an entry-level or executive position, you can increase your chances for selection as a temporary employee by revising your resume. Highlight your experience and emphasize projects you've handled rather than how long you worked with former employers. Market yourself as an interim professional as Paige O'Conner did: "After I lost my job I had no idea what I wanted to do. Fortunately, I'd been taking classes in night school. I marketed myself to several employment agencies as an interim employee in the information systems area. Even though I was short 12 credits for my degree in computer science, they saw me as someone with good placement potential. I had a great temporary job within a week that offered flex-time so I could continue going to school. Upon graduation I was offered a full-time job which I enjoy. I've been here almost 9 years thanks to a temporary opportunity with permanent possibilities, something I almost didn't try for because I didn't think anything would come of it."

Myth #24

It's okay to use the informational interview to ask about a job.

Reality

Your objective in an informational interview is to learn more about a particular career or business—not to get a job offer.

Discussion

If you're not sure about your career path or if you want more information about where to look for job opportunities in your field, schedule an informational interview. Ideally, someone you know can give you the name of a business person to contact. If you don't have this type of contact, you'll need to search out the information yourself.

When you phone, mention the name of the person who referred you. Be sure to state early in the conversation that you're not asking for a job, but requesting an interview to gather information and advice.

Plan ahead just as you would for a job interview. Develop a list of questions you want to ask. Prepare a brief history about yourself and your goals.

Once someone has agreed to meet with you for an informational interview, observe the same guidelines that you would follow for a job interview:

- Arrive on time.
- Dress professionally.
- Behave in a businesslike manner.

The informational interview should follow this basic outline:

- Introduce yourself. Give an overall summary of the information you need and why you're asking the person to help you.
- Present a brief biography (not more than two minutes).
- Ask questions. Find out which companies are hiring people at your level, and try to get the names of others you can contact.
- Summarize and close. Once you have all the data you need, briefly summarize the information you discussed, as you understand it.
- Thank the interviewer for his time and willingness to meet with you.
- Do not ask the interviewer for a job.

After the interview, be sure to follow up with a thank you letter just as you would after a formal interview.

Eddie Strauss, vice president of store operations in a retail setting, offered this additional advice: "I've managed people for 30 years and hired a lot as well. I never objected to meeting with candidates to offer suggestions. However, I don't appreciate people who try to pressure me into giving them a job. For example, a recent college graduate got my name by networking. He called and asked if he could meet for an informational interview. When he got to my office I found out he really wasn't interested in information. He wanted me to find him a job within my company. I felt 'used.' I also didn't feel comfortable recommending him to a colleague who had a job opening for which the candidate may have been qualified."

Think of the informational interview as a "non-interview interview." The point of the interview is to gather information. It offers an opportunity to learn more about a business or industry while getting a chance to meet someone who may consider hiring you in the future or recommending you to others.

Myth #25

The best way to find a job is to broadcast to the largest number of people possible.

Reality

Your job search should employ an organized approach that includes contacting people who are most likely to help accelerate your job search.

Discussion

There's a difference between just "telling everyone" and "networking." Most people who tell everyone they're unemployed tend to verbalize it as a feeling of distress over the situation. They give others the general impression that they're primarily looking for sympathy and comfort. In networking, while you share with others that you're unemployed (or interested in changing jobs), you approach it in an organized manner. You have a goal, and you're looking for information and suggestions rather than sympathy. The following two examples illustrate the difference.

Examples: Malcolm Brown lost his job due to a company lay-off. He hadn't had to job hunt in over 10 years and was upset about the prospect of looking for work. He told everyone he came in contact with about the unfairness of the situation, and how much he dreaded looking for a job. When someone asked what type of work might interest him, he mumbled that he didn't really know and wasn't sure where he'd find work. He got a lot of sympathy and verbal encouragement, but that was all.

Jim Hunter also lost his job due to a lay-off. Although initially as discouraged as Brown, he quickly took a more upbeat approach. He decided that he was willing to explore another area outside his previous field. He registered with the state employment office and several private employment agencies. When he talked to friends, neighbors, and other acquaintances about his situation, he tried to sound positive. He contacted a few business colleagues he felt close to and let them know he was available. It took 4 months, but he found a new job through a contact who had heard about an opening. In addition, he felt better about himself and his situation because he took charge of his job search.

Use your energy to network, not just tell people you're out of work.

Example: "Look under every rock and you shall find," claims Edna Peoples. She's a former job seeker who finally decided that telling everyone she knew that she was unemployed was not a good idea. "I initially wanted to tell the world I was unemployed, because I thought that strategy would help me get a job quicker. I guess I thought people would feel sorry for me and hire me. Then, a career counselor set me straight. She taught me the importance of knowing what I wanted in a job and how to go about finding it."

Peoples shared an excerpt adapted from *The Complete Job Interview Handbook* by John J. Marcus. She found this helpful in getting started.

If You Are Unemployed and Need Interviews Immediately

- Telephone potential employers.
- Make personal contacts.
- Talk to employment agencies (only if an agency specializes in your field).
- Make telephone calls in response to advertisements.
- Send broadcast letters (especially if contacting a large number of companies).

If You Are Employed and Require Confidentiality

- Make personal contacts and use third-party correspondence (particularly if you are contacting companies in your own industry).
- Try media advertisements.
- Contact executive search firms.
- Contact employment agencies (only if an agency specializes in your field).
- Send broadcast letters.

If You Want to Make a Career Change

- Make personal contacts.
- Conduct informational interviews.
- Use third-party correspondence (through direct mail as well as answering ads).

If You Are Seeking Advancement in the Same Field

- Make personal contacts.
- Telephone potential employers.
- Contact employment agencies (only if an agency specializes in the field).
- Send broadcast letters.
- Try media advertisements.
- Contact executive search firms.

If You Are a Junior-Level Job-Seeker

- Take advantage of college and alumni placement offices.
- Make personal contacts.
- Conduct informational interviews.
- Try media advertisements.
- Telephone potential employers.
- Contact employment agencies.
- Send broadcast letters.

If You Are a Senior-Level Job-Seeker

- Make personal contacts.
- Try media advertisements.
- Send broadcast letters.
- Contact executive search firms.

If You Wish to Relocate

- Send broadcast letters.
- Make personal contacts (if you have them in the desired locale).
- Contact employment agencies and media advertisements (only if you have exceptional qualifications).

Peoples fell into the first category—*If You Are Unemployed and Need Interviews Immediately.* She decided what kind of work she wanted, got organized, and started contacting individuals and companies that matched her job requirements. Two months later she accepted a position she enjoys in the health care industry.

Peoples concluded, "I'm very happy with my final decision to work in a rehabilitation center. I can put my experience and talents to work here and I feel appreciated for even the smallest things I do. The patients are great and keep me on my toes. My boss is supportive and encourages me to challenge myself. How I approached my job search had a lot to do with how I feel about my work today."

Myth #26

Most job openings appear in newspaper advertisements.

Reality

Approximately 25 to 30 percent of all available jobs are advertised in the newspaper. The other 70 to 75 percent are part of the "hidden" market.

Discussion

Your challenge is to find the "hidden" market opportunities through other means. Most people still consider networking the best way to make contacts. Some of the most popular networking approaches include:

- Initiating and building your own networking circle of contacts. (Ideally, you did this before you became unemployed). It's always nice to have good business contacts when you need them.
- Attending professional association meetings.
- Participating in activities of job-lead organizations. (See Appendix C for a list of resources.)

- Volunteering for community service work with organizations such as United Way, Junior Achievement, Boys/Girls Clubs of America, Habitat for Humanity, etc. It's a great way to help others as well as make business contacts.
- Participating on a community task force.
- Meeting people through religious organizations, your children's school, alumni associations, or neighborhood social clubs.
- Contacting your college alumni/alumnae placement office. They often maintain job banks of current listings. They match graduates' resumes against these openings and forward them to the appropriate companies.

It's important that you meet people. Contact everyone you know. Renew old acquaintances. Don't ask them for a job or put pressure on them; simply ask if they know anyone who might know where there's a job opportunity that might be of interest to you.

Example: When Sue Beal was downsized by her employer, she prepared a flyer "advertising" her skills and work experience. She not only distributed it to people she knew, but put it under the doormat of every unit in the condominium complex where she lived. A neighbor had a contact for her, which led to a job interview and a salary offer that was above what she had earned previously.

Beal's advice is: "Talk to people you know. Tell them you're looking for a job. Don't be embarrassed; most people have been through job loss themselves and are willing to help. While you're networking with folks you know, contact some you don't know. There really is a 'hidden' job market, and it's every job hunter's responsibility to penetrate it."

As you begin your search, keep an open mind about the contacts and resources available to you. The newspaper is only one avenue for finding your next job opportunity. Waiting for the telephone to ring could mean a long time between job interviews. Be creative and help yourself. If you don't, who will?

Myth #27

The Human Resources Department is the best place to start your job search.

Reality

One of the primary jobs of the Human Resources Department is to screen *out* applicants.

Discussion

Send your resume to the person in the organization who has the power to hire you. Consider mailing a marketing letter to the president of the company. He or she will probably see it and pass it on to others. Your letter, and you, will get more exposure that way. To avoid elimination from the competition, focus your efforts on contacting decision-makers.

If the first person you contact in an organization says the company has no job openings, don't automatically give up. Make calls or send resumes to some of the people you've identified with impressive titles. Managers, especially in large companies, don't always tell each other what's available in their departments.

If your contact tells you that you'll have to talk to Human Resources, say, "Thanks, I'd be glad to contact them. Who should I ask to speak to in the Human Resources Department?" Then continue by asking if you may use their name as an introduction when you call. You might also ask if they know whether there's a specific job opening.

Lois Hunt, a human resources manager for her family's business, had this to say: "We get hundreds of resumes, applications, and phone calls every year. We have a good reputation in the community and a lot of people want to work for us. I screen resumes and applications quickly against the job requirements. There have been situations where applicants have contacted my father or one of my brothers directly. When one of them comes to me and tells me he's found the perfect candidate to fill a job opening, I say, 'Great,' because it saves me the trouble of finding someone to meet their needs."

Hunt also said that human resource managers might be a roadblock for those seeking employment. She offered this additional advice:

- Find out who the decision-maker is in the company in which you have an interest.
- Call and ask for an informational interview.
- Dress professionally for the interview, regardless of the position for which you're applying. There's no excuse for sloppy dress, dirty fingernails, unkempt hair, unpolished shoes, too much makeup, or a mini-skirt in any interview, including an informational interview.
- Show interest; ask for advice. The decision-maker will figure out that you're looking for employment. Don't put pressure on him or her by asking for a job.
- Respect the time of the person who's speaking with you. Overstaying your welcome could cost you a job lead (or even a job).
- Express appreciation for his or her time at the end of the interview.
- Immediately follow up with a thank you letter to every person who took the time to meet with you. Some job seekers overlook this important step. Failure to show appreciation can also cost you an opportunity.

Keep in mind an important point mentioned throughout this book: The informational interview is for the purpose of obtaining information. Although it would be wonderful if the informational interview led to a job interview (and hopefully to a job offer), don't ask for an informational interview and then try to turn it into a job interview. You'll do more damage than good for your career.

Myth #28

Job fairs seldom lead to job offers.

Reality

Although most job fairs offer only a few minutes with each company representative, they're a great place to network and gather information about potential employers. Job fairs *can* lead to job offers.

Discussion

Learn how to psyche yourself up for job fairs. Remember these tips:

- Plan for a full day of activity.
- Find out which companies are going to be present and allow enough time in your schedule to see all of them.
- Do some advance research on the companies you want to visit at the fair.
- Practice what you want to say. You'll need a two-minute "commercial" highlighting your background and skills.
- Dress to impress. A job fair is just as much an interview as a face-to-face interview on-site with a company representative.

- Hand out your business card to other job seekers as well as prospective employers.
- Take extra copies of your resume and leave one with each company representative.
- Use an attaché case (or small briefcase) to keep your resumes neat and clean, and to store material you collect.
- Don't go to an employer's booth with food, a beverage, or cigarette in your hand. Wait for a break to refresh yourself.
- Participate in workshops on job-search topics of interest.
- Network with other job seekers. Everyone you meet is a potential job lead.
- Take mini breaks throughout the day. You don't want to appear worn-out or uninterested because you're tired of talking and standing.
- Pick up business cards and printed information so you have reminders of companies and representatives with whom you spoke.
- Follow up with thank you letters to company representatives who interviewed you.
- If you have time, talk to those companies that you aren't particularly interested in. You might still get a job lead.

When you write your thank you letter, be sure to remind the recruiter of your conversation at the job fair and your qualifications. Remember, each recruiter may meet many candidates at the fair, so try to include an item in your letter that will help to spark the recruiter's memory. In the letter, express your interest in setting up an appointment for an on-site interview.

It's also a good idea to make notes in your job journal about what you'd like to do differently at the next job fair. Note what you felt worked or didn't work, or tips you learned about how to use the job fair to your best advantage.

A job fair provides an excellent opportunity to both candidates and recruiters to make that important initial, face-to-face contact.

Lastly, Jenny Hall, an on-campus recruiter for her employer had this to add: "We hire roughly 35 percent of all new employees from candidates we meet at job fairs; we wish that figure were higher. I meet people at job fairs who haven't prepared and violate one or more of the basic rules for interviewing. My advice is to be ready for anything, up to and including a job offer as a result of your efforts."

Myth #29

It's difficult using the Internet to conduct a job search.

Reality

Job hunting in cyberspace isn't much different from using conventional methods.

Discussion

Limiting your job search to checking the classified ads, papering the country with your resume, and hitting up your business contacts for referrals means you're missing out on one of the best career tools available—the World Wide Web.

The Internet is a great place to start a job search. The amount of information available may surprise you. Resources include job banks, recruiters, temporary agencies, and resources for recent college graduates. You can even use a service that will create a list of potential employers for you.

Start with The Monster Board (http://www.monster.com). It has a database of more than 50,000 job postings. There are listings in a variety of categories including finance, health care, sales, engineering, information systems, hospitality, retail, and more.

In addition, you can refine your search by location, job title, or other criteria by using Career Mosaic (http://www.careermosaic.com) and Yahoo! (http://classifieds.yahoo.com).

Many on-line job banks, such as Job Hunt at (http://www.job-hunt.org) offer regional search capabilities.

Try Best Jobs in the USA Today (http://Bestjobusa.com) to access newspaper ads, resume repository, and job events.

You may also want to try Career Net at (http://www.careers.org), which links to regional and state job banks across the country.

You can also search on-line classified and business sections of local newspapers. Career Path (http://www.careerpath.com) compiles newspaper employment ads from more than 50 major U.S. cities.

Best Jobs USA, Online Career Center, Career Magazine (http://www.careermag.com), or E-Span (http://www.espan.com) are like mini-libraries. Along with job listings, there are opportunities to place your resume, get information on a particular company, and gather advice from career counselors.

America's Job Bank (http://www.ajb.dni.us), a product of the U.S. Department of Labor, posts more than 500,000 jobs each month. Ninety-five percent of these jobs are in the private sector.

Some additional on-line resources include:

- Asia-Net (http://www.asia-net.com)
- Black Collegian Online (http://www.blackcollegian.com)
- CollegeCentral (http://www.collegecentral.com)
- HeadHunter.com (http://www.headhunter.com)
- HireWire (http//www.hirewire.com)
- I-Search (http://www.isearch.com)
- Job Direct (http://www.jobdirect.com)
- JobMarket (http://www.jobmarket.com)
- JobTrak (http://www.jobtrak.com)
- Jobweb (http://www.jobweb.org)
- MercuryCenter (http://www.sjmercury.com)
- National Urban League (http://www.nul.org)
- NationJob (http://www.nationjob.com)
- Professional Job Network (http://www.professionaljobnetwork.com)
- Restrac (http://www.restrac.com)

- Resumix (http://www.resumix.com)
- Talent Alliance (http://www.talentalliance.org)
- Washington Post (http://www.washingtonpost.com)
- Women's Wire (http://www.womenswire.com/work)
- Working (http://www.townonline.com/working)

Thousands of companies post job openings on their Web sites. There is also a growing list of specialized want ad sites. The question that remains for the job seeker is how to make the best use of the existing resources.

Benefits of using the Internet to conduct a job search include efficiency (you can use key words to speed your search) and the ability to easily research out-of-town locations (you can read the classified section of most major papers on-line).

Although most experts agree that the Internet should be part of your job search, here's a word of caution: Do not ignore the proven techniques of networking, informational interviews, submitting resumes, etc. They still work and that's how the majority of people still find jobs today.

Myth #30

Networking is sleazy.

Reality

When done properly networking is a great way to build relationships that lead to job offers.

Discussion

"Suck up," "fake it 'til you make it," become a "political animal," and "schmooze" are terms sometimes used for networking. Unfortunately, the art of meeting people for the purpose of doing business occasionally has a bad reputation. Don't let it discourage you or cause you to feel embarrassed about meeting new people. As long as you don't compromise your integrity you'll be fine.

The traditional definition for networking is: "The activity of contacting friends, colleagues, neighbors, and family members to find out about unadvertised job opportunities." If everything goes as planned, your networking contacts will tell others, who themselves will tell others, that you're looking for a job. The network will expand like a web.

One of the benefits of networking is that you can find out about job openings before they're advertised. This may enable you to out-hustle your competition.

Start by listing the names of *everyone* you know. You could have several hundred names that include people such as business associates, friends, neighbors, child's music teacher, minister, etc. These people are your "primary" contacts. Call them. Meet with them. Talk to them. Ask them if they know anyone who might have an interest in someone with your qualifications. The names they give you are your "secondary" contacts—people who know your primary contacts. Call them. Meet with them. Talk to them. Ask them for referrals, the objective of your networking activities. Try to get at least one referral from every person you contact.

In addition, don't overlook the obvious. People you interact with every day could lead you to a great job opportunity. If you're a recent college graduate, don't forget classmates, faculty members, and your friends' parents.

Example: Craig Espinoza successfully used networking to find a new job after he lost his job as a customer service representative for a software company. His supervisor caught him making personal telephone calls on company time. His employer accepted no excuses, fired him, and Espinoza was out of a job. His first reaction was shock and disbelief. He had been "employee of the year" the previous year and thought nothing could tarnish his reputation.

Espinoza started his search by networking with members of his bowling team. He used his contacts as a Boy Scout leader and also networked with members of his church. He used the Internet to find leads, and also e-mailed friends about his job search. He applied for positions he found in newspapers and professional journals. After 2 months of looking full-time he had two offers. Espinoza accepted the offer that he felt was the best fit for him, has been in his new job 3 years, and has earned two promotions. And he's no longer making personal calls on company time.

Consider networking at:

- Job fairs.
- Professional association meetings.
- Alumni conferences.
- Outplacement firms.
- Recruitment agencies.

- Parties and social events.
- Volunteer organizations in which you're active.
- Neighborhood gatherings.
- Church activities.

You don't have to be a baby-kissing politician or come across like a high-pressure salesperson. Meeting someone through a mutual friend is like a seal of approval. "Pre-approved" contacts are an accepted way of doing business.

When you use networking, keep in mind that you have some responsibilities to the people who've assisted you in your search. Don't make a contact wish he'd never helped you by being pushy or rude with someone he or she has referred you to or helped you contact. Don't expect your contacts to magically "make" someone hire you either. Never blame your contacts if a job interview doesn't produce a job offer.

Notify your main contacts promptly (within 2 weeks) when you've found a job. Write each person a thank you letter advising them of the good news, and express appreciation for their help in your job search.

Networking is a two-way process; give others help when they ask for it. People you've assisted will have more interest in helping you in the future. Helping others can also help you feel better about networking yourself, particularly if you've felt slightly uneasy when doing so.

Myth #31

Long-distance job hunting is a waste of time.

Reality

Job hunting from a distance may make it more difficult to identify leads, make contacts, and conduct interviews, but it's possible to be successful if you have a plan.

Discussion

There are two main reasons for long-distance job hunting. Maybe you have family in another city and have decided you want to live closer to them. Or you visited an area and decided it seemed like a nice place to settle down someday. Whatever your reason for wanting to relocate, if you would like to make a move to a city where you've never worked, you'll need to gather as much information about that area as possible. The more familiar you are with the area, the greater likelihood you'll succeed in finding a job opportunity there.

The second reason for considering long-distance job hunting is that you decide job openings in your current location are limited. Unless you don't care where you live as long as you have a job, you'll also want to take time to gather information about possible new locations. The time to do that is before you submit resumes or make telephone contacts.

Follow these tips to help make your long-distance job hunting a little easier:

- Identify people you know who live in your target city.
- Let your contacts know by letter, telephone, and/or e-mail that you plan to relocate.
- Order the Yellow Pages and the Chamber of Commerce Directory of Businesses and Industries.
- Practice your telephone skills and plan what you want to say.
- Contact venture capital firms that may have job opportunities in your target city.
- Place a "position wanted" ad in the newspaper.
- Contact your local public library for information about companies in your target city.
- Subscribe to local newspapers; in addition to the Sunday classifieds, you'll get more information about the city in which you plan to live.
- If you belong to a professional association with a national membership, find out the names of members in your target area. Use your membership directory to network.
- If you're on a limited budget, make your initial contact by mail. Follow up by telephone.
- Search on the Internet for Web sites that highlight the area or list local newspaper classifieds. (See information in Myth #29.)
- Purchase a copy of *The Directory of Executive Recruiters* (1-800-531-0007) to get names of recruiters who operate in your target city and industry.
- Visit the city in which you plan to relocate. Do so more than once. Arrange to meet with your networking contacts.
- Stay in touch. The biggest mistake you can make is to let your contacts and leads forget you because you didn't stay in contact.

Keep in mind that you're not alone. Research indicates that the number of job hunters who are willing to move for a new position increases each year.

You'll also want to consider the cost-of-living index in another city before you make a commitment.

Example: Kathryn Allen got an out-of-town job offer with a salary that sounded great, until compared to the cost of living in that area. In reality, the offer didn't constitute a "step up" but came closer to being a "step down" economically. She still accepted the offer, because of the long-term potential she saw in the job, but she made the move with a clear understanding of the financial agreement into which she was entering. "I couldn't be happier with my decision to relocate even though the money in my pocket wasn't what I had originally anticipated. However, today I look back on my career and realize that moving was worth the initial sacrifice because it fit my long-term career objectives."

Myth #32

The best jobs are in high-growth industries.

Reality

There are good opportunities in every industry, in every field.

Discussion

Regardless of the industry, you'll find competition for good jobs. Your goal is to find those businesses that have opportunities. Some are obvious while others are more difficult to find. You may not be aware of job openings, but they're available.

The service industry, for example, is booming. Hotels and restaurants, retail and grocery stores are always looking for employees. Research organizations, non-profits, manufacturers, and construction companies are also hiring.

On the other hand, despite the growth in the computer industry, companies like Digital Equipment Corporation, IBM, Wang, and others considered to be in a hot industry have had major re-organizations. Even companies in fast-growth areas have their share of problems.

Example: Ted Bock, a job seeker, wasted time trying to get a job with one of several well-known companies in an area that's perceived as growing. "I had it in my head that I was going to use my degree in public health administration if it was the last thing I did," said Bock. Everyone knows the health care field is hot, but they've also had cutbacks. As it turned out, I'm not a hospital administrator, as I thought I would be. I accepted a great job offer with an insurance company in their marketing department. The job's a little removed from what I expected to be doing, but I love it."

Bock is an example of someone who started out looking at job opportunities only in the obvious places. Although initially disappointed in his job search, he broadened his interests (while still selling his strengths to employers) and ended up in a rewarding job.

Example: Lyle Sawyer had this to say: "I was a systems analyst in a growing company, in a hot industry. However, I was burned out from the long hours. There was no balance in my life. I moved into manufacturing with a small company and today I'm in charge of their distribution center. I use both my people skills and my computer skills. The years I spent as a systems analyst were not wasted. I simply needed a change. A new job in a different industry has been the answer to my frustration with my last position and I didn't have any trouble finding it."

Small businesses, especially those that are growing, can also provide likely places for jobs. Sometimes the owner or manager has been thinking about hiring another person, but just hasn't taken the time to begin the search. Your call or visit may remind them of their need. The good news is that you're there and interested in their company, which gives you a distinct advantage.

Don't overlook career fields or companies that aren't considered in a "hot" industry. The hidden job market offers a gold mine of opportunity for those who are willing to take the time to explore and network with people who may know of job openings in areas previously unconsidered.

Myth #33

Companies don't hire during the December holidays.

Reality

December is actually a good month to search for a job.

Discussion

Don't lose momentum when you turn the calendar page to December. This isn't the season to become complacent. It's a time to give your best effort so you can start the new year on a positive note.

Job hunters are conditioned to believe there are certain times during the year when companies aren't interviewing. They believe that businesses close during the holidays or employers don't want to bother with interviewing during this time. This may be the case with some organizations, but many never stop recruiting.

Consider the following:

- You have less competition during the holidays. Other job seekers think it's a bad time and take a break.

- It's a good time to network because most people are more sociable during the holidays.
- Human resource and senior managers are in the office while many of their support staff are on vacation. It's often easier to make contact because they answer their own telephones.

In addition, it's okay to network at holiday parties, just don't ask for a job. Say something like, "I'm looking for a new opportunity. May I give you my business card?" Then, follow up 7 to 10 days later.

Keep in mind that December holidays mean different things to different companies, according to employees' religious or cultural beliefs. If you're not sure about the appropriate holiday greeting, don't use one. A simple, "Good morning" or "Good-bye," will be sufficient.

According to Hank Drew, vice president of human resources for Boyd & Associates, December is a great month to look for job opportunities: "Just be gracious and don't appear pushy, especially at social events. Network and apply for any job that appears to be a match. You'll be surprised how many companies interview during the holiday season. Our company is a good example. We've made some of our best hiring decisions in December. We have more time to talk to candidates and it also gives them a chance to learn more about us. My advice to job seekers is to keep the momentum going by interviewing any time of the year until you find a job."

Myth #34

If companies aren't hiring,
there's nothing you can do about it.

Reality

Sometimes it's necessary to create a demand for your services.

Discussion

It's great to find organizations that have job openings, but if they don't you can attempt to do something to get them interested in you.

You will always use the conventional methods for job hunting. Writing a resume, networking, contacting prospective employers, and preparing for interviewers is important. However, when you're in a situation where you want to work for a specific company and it appears they have no openings, it's time to try something new.

Follow these steps to create your own job opportunity:

- *Step #1—Research your target company.* You'll need more in-depth information if you want to create an opening for yourself. Research takes time, but it's necessary. You'll want to know as much as possible about the organization's financial history, key personnel, and their functions, especially the department within which you want to work.

If it's a publicly owned company, you can request a copy of their annual report. The Public Relations or Human Resources Department should be able to help. For more details, request the 10-K (annual report that's filed by publicly held companies with the U.S. Securities and Exchange Commission). This information can also be obtained from the Securities and Exchange Commission's Web site. Ask for a recent Proxy that provides information about the firm's directors and officers. Privately held companies will not have information to give the public. However, you can ask for other publications. Call your local library and Chamber of Commerce. Use your personal computer to access additional information. For instance, many private companies now maintain their own Web sites.

If your interest is in working for a specific subsidiary or division of a company, get similar information about them.

- *Step #2—After you've completed your research, develop an outline of the organization's financial history,* including:

    —Sales.

    —Profit.

    —Expertise.

    —Assets.

    —Liabilities.

    —Stockholder's equity.

    —Stock prices.

Look at how these figures have fluctuated over time, and consider suggested future trends. Your goal in research of this kind is to determine the health of the business. Once you know that, you can make a decision about whether or not you still want to pursue a job with them. If profits are down, you may want to continue your search elsewhere.

Once you've determined you want to work for a particular company, it's time to try to gain entry. This may take some persistence, but you have several avenues to explore:

- Networking—Do you have a contact who might introduce you or give you a referral? See if you can arrange an informational interview.

- Personnel Department—Many companies will accept resumes/applications even if not hiring at the moment.
- Recruiter—Contact a recruiting agency, tell them of your interest in XYZ Corporation, and ask for an appointment.
- Telephone—Make telephone contact with people in the company, as mentioned in other myths. The key here is to let them know that you specifically want to work for their organization and why, and what you feel you could bring to the company.

Sometimes companies have job openings that they haven't advertised or don't plan to advertise immediately. Your call may come at a time when they're just beginning to consider the creation of a new position. Even if nothing happens immediately, you've made the managers aware of your interest.

When you're trying to create a place for yourself in a company that's "not hiring," you have to make them aware that you've taken the time to learn about their company and convince them that hiring you would benefit them.

Example: Erin Turner wanted to work for a specific consumer products company. She tried cold-calling, mailing resumes, and networking through friends. It wasn't until she met a woman at a cocktail party that an opportunity became apparent. Turner had a graphics design background. She explained what she was doing for her current employer and her desire to make a job change into the consumer products industry, in particular, the company for whom the woman she met worked. Although there were no job openings at the time in the Graphics Department, Turner was able to convince them that she had a lot to offer and that what she could do for them would justify her salary. They agreed to give her a chance. Now, three years later, she's the manager of the department. "I was assertive in pursuing a job with them even though they didn't have a job opening. I refused to give up and it worked. Some of it was luck, but most of it was persistence."

Some final words of advice were offered by Regina Tully, a sales manager: "I've hired more people than I can count over the last 25 years. The few exceptions who really researched the company prior to the interview could be counted on two hands. I'm not talking about basic research, but candidates who had extensive knowledge of our company and products. Some knew more than the people who interviewed them. Those were the folks who got my attention and the jobs."

Myth #35

Researching a company isn't as important as how you present your skills and abilities in a personal interview.

Reality

To prepare effectively for the interview, you need to know as much as possible about the organization.

Discussion

Interviewers perceive researching the company as a critical factor in evaluating candidates. A candidate who hasn't taken time to research a prospective employer enters the interview at a disadvantage. How does someone convince an interviewer that he or she is the right person for the job if they're unfamiliar with the company, its products, or goals? Such lack of knowledge also tells the interviewer the candidate either: (1) wasn't savvy enough to realize the importance of researching the company; or (2) just didn't care enough. Either assumption hurts the candidate.

There's no reason for a candidate to neglect researching a company prior to an interview. Numerous directories and reference materials are available.

You can find these publications at business or university libraries. Chambers of Commerce also frequently publish directories of local businesses and organizations.

Before you begin your research, consider the following:

- Is the company publicly owned? It's generally easier to gather information on these companies than privately held companies.
- It's usually easier to find information on corporations than about their subsidiaries or divisions.
- The larger and more well-known the company, the easier to locate information.
- Check the date on your information. Sometimes a library has outdated information.
- No one library has everything. Check school libraries, Chambers of Commerce, and government offices.
- See if your library has access to CD-ROM products and on-line database search services.

Also review the search information given in Myth #34. If you're preparing for an interview for an existing job, you won't need to conduct as in-depth a search for information as the person seeking to create a position. However, you can still use some of the resources listed in Myth #34 to prepare.

Remember the key question: "How do you expect to convince an interviewer you're the right person for the job if you're not familiar with the company and what it does?"

Tim Thomas, a human resource manager, offered this advice, "I expect candidates to know something about our company. Although we're privately held, information is available on our Web site. I expect sharp job seekers to come prepared for the interview. Job skills are very important, but candidates who want to stand out above their competition need to know something about our 100-year-old history and what we do in the industry. Candidates who know these things definitely have an edge."

Myth #36

*Recruiters are in business to find
employment for job seekers.*

Reality

Recruiters work for client companies, not individuals.

Discussion

It's important to understand the difference between a retained search firm and a contingency search firm. A retained search firm works exclusively for employers who contract with them to find candidates. A contingency firm will represent individuals seeking placement. A retained firm usually handles only senior-level assignments. Contingency recruiters handle primarily middle to lower level placements.

The chance of getting a job through a recruiter, headhunter, or employment agency of any kind is variable. In other words, don't rely exclusively on agencies as a method for finding a job.

In most cases, recruiters or headhunters will be interested in you only if they know of an actual opening that calls for someone with your background and qualifications.

However, there are several strategies you can use to develop a relationship with recruiters:

1. Identify the recruiters who specialize in your industry and profession. More than 1,000 are listed by specialty and location in *The Directory of Executive Recruiters* ($44.95, Kennedy Publications, 1-800-531-0007). (Software version is also available for $195.00.)
2. Target mailings by sending your resume only to recruiters who specialize in your field. New technology makes it easy for employment agencies to scan and store your information. Many recruiters will be happy to receive your resume as long as it's in their field.
3. Network to meet recruiters and headhunters. Get people who know them to personally introduce you. Cold calling is seldom productive.
4. Attend conferences sponsored by one of the professional association(s) in your field and meet recruiters there. Many recruiters participate in order to scout talent. Introduce yourself. Tell them you'd be glad to help them find good people in your specialty area. Recruiters live by referrals.

What should you expect when you contact a recruiter or they contact you?

- If the recruiter asks for money, end the conversation. Most agencies receive payment from their corporate clients.
- If they want you to sign a contract or pay a fee, find someone else to help you.

Recruiters who are hunting for just the right candidate to fill a high position within a client company do not limit their search to the unemployed. They will contact an employed individual to determine his or her interest.

If you receive a call of this nature, but are not familiar with the name of the recruiter, ask for a telephone number and call the recruiter back. Don't take a chance that someone from your company or its investors is posing as a recruiter to see whether or not you'll jump ship.

Myth #37

When questioning recruiters about job openings, you run the risk of alienating them.

Reality

Any time you're working with a recruiter, you have the right to ask and have answered any questions that will help you understand the job opportunity.

Discussion

During the initial conversation, recruiters won't give you the name of the company, but will give a brief description of the type of work and the position they're seeking to fill. Ask the following questions of recruiters to help you decide if the job they're trying to fill is right for you:

- Can you provide a description of the company and information about its position in the industry?
- What's the job title and what are the general job responsibilities?
- To whom does the position report?

- How long has the position been available?
- Why is the job open?
- How many other candidates are under consideration?
- Why didn't they fill the position from within the organization?
- What is the typical career path?
- Would the job require relocating?
- Would the position require extensive travel?
- What is the compensation package?

If the recruiter is good, he or she will have the answers to your questions.

*   *   *

Obviously there are different considerations depending on whether you're employed or unemployed. If a recruiter calls you at your current job and you're interested, ask him or her to call you at home or meet away from your office in order to discuss the above questions.

If you determine you have no interest in the opportunity, you might offer the names of people you think would be interested in the position. You may need a friend in the recruiting world in the future.

Example: Louise Hopper learned from her mistakes: "I used to get calls from headhunters at least once a week. My background is in credit and collections and there always seems to be a need for people with my skills. In the past, I got very annoyed when they called. I was rude. I could have just as easily said: 'I'm not interested, but thanks for calling me' instead of responding abruptly or hanging up before they had finished their first sentence. Then one day I found myself looking for another job. I felt like a fool calling these same recruiters to ask for help. My advice is at the minimum be pleasant. If you have time for friendship, that's even better. You never know when you'll be looking for a job again."

Myth #38

All employment agencies are alike.

Reality

Employment agencies differ according to location (region of the country) as well as the level of job openings they fill.

Discussion

A good choice in an agency can prove invaluable in helping you find a job. A poor choice can bring lots of problems. For example: Agencies receive payment through commission. Therefore, the quicker they fill the vacancy, the sooner they get paid. Their focus may not be as much on finding the right opportunity for you as on finding a job you're willing to accept. Be sure you understand the parameters of your agreement before you get started.

It is helpful to understand the differences between agencies and their services.

Employment Agencies

Employment agencies fill primarily full-time positions. The employer and/or employee pays the fee, which is generally 20–25 percent of the candidate's starting salary. As a candidate you may never meet the agency representative in person because the representative usually handles everything by telephone, especially if you're conducting a long-distance search.

Executive Recruiters

Executive recruiters work on either a retainer or contingency basis to place entry-level to mid-level managers. Executive recruiters charge their corporate clients up to 30 percent of the candidate's first year's salary, plus expenses.

Executive Search Firms

An employer's answer to filling an especially difficult position could be an executive search firm. They (headhunters) work to fill senior-level positions for client companies. Some specialize by industry or type of position. Some firms are local while others have several locations and therefore have access to a large computer database of applicants. They typically work on a retainer. Fees are 30–35 percent of the new hire's first year's salary plus bonuses and any expenses associated with the search. The hiring company pays these fees. If you're highly specialized or at the executive level, executive search firms may be interested in you.

State Employment Services

State agencies provide referral services at no cost to employers or candidates. They place candidates from entry- to senior-level, employed as well as unemployed. However, most of the jobs available through these services are in the entry- to mid-level salary range.

                    *   *   *

Before making that first call to an agency:

- Plan the scope of the search and whether you want the agency to conduct a local, regional, national, or international search.
- Be prepared with the information the agency will ask you to provide regarding desired benefits and salary, including bonus, commission, etc. In addition, you can expect a good recruiter to want a complete

profile of you, your qualifications, and what you're looking for, before
beginning the search.

- Determine how much time you're willing to give the agency to conduct a thorough search. Some agencies will want you to commit to
  working exclusively with them.

In addition, consider these points to make sure agencies don't take advantage of you:

- Check references on the agencies in which you have an interest.
- Agencies are licensed by the states in which they operate. Make sure
  the license is current and in good standing.
- With rare exception, you shouldn't have to pay a fee to get a job.
- Don't sign any contracts or agreements to pay for services unless you
  understand what you're signing.

THE INTERVIEW AND BEYOND

Job seekers need to prepare for what they'll encounter during the interview. Skillful interviewers will ask questions on a variety of work-related subjects. They'll probe your past performance in an effort to find clues to how you'll perform in the future. They might ask you something that's considered inappropriate or even illegal. How you respond could make the difference between a bright new future and another rejection letter.

The average prospective employer will spend 65–75 percent of the total interview time exploring your technical qualifications for the position. He or she will also want to find out how you plan to help the company achieve its objectives and whether or not you have the skills and abilities to do so. The interviewer will use your answers to make a judgment regarding your "fit" with the organization's culture.

You, of course, will want to evaluate the interviewer and the company as well. Note body language. Listen carefully to what's being said as well as what's not being said to you during the interview. Is this the place you want to work, or do you get the feeling something's not quite right about this position?

In addition, keep in mind that getting the initial interview is just a first step. The next step is being invited back for a second interview. Rarely will you close a deal for a new job without a second interview, maybe even a third and a fourth.

Part III is the most important part of this book. You'll find suggestions to help you position yourself competitively in the job market. You'll also get advice on how to approach some of the most challenging parts of the job search, including how to coach references and negotiate salary and benefits.

The myths discussed in Part III are:

39. Some job interviews are a waste of time.
40. You probably won't be asked to participate in a video conference interview.
41. The interview begins when you meet the interviewer.
42. Employers are more interested in what you have to say than what you wear to the interview.
43. When asked what kind of job you're looking for, it's acceptable to say, "Anything that's available."
44. Your goal in the interview is to share as much as you can about yourself.
45. An effective way to let the interviewer know you're relaxed is by telling a joke.
46. When asked about your weaknesses, answer honestly.
47. Never ask questions in the interview; that's the interviewer's job.
48. Employers are willing to sacrifice technical expertise to attract candidates.
49. Employers know better than to ask inappropriate or illegal questions.
50. It's best to share your salary expectations when you meet the interviewer to avoid misunderstandings later.
51. There's no way to prepare for pre-employment tests.
52. Follow up after an interview may give the impression you're desperate for a job.
53. Expressing gratitude in a thank you letter is enough.
54. Most companies don't check references.
55. Personal references are as useful as work-related references.
56. If you didn't get along with your former boss, you'll get a bad reference.
57. If you're invited for a meal, you can assume the job is yours.
58. The company's first offer is their best and last offer.
59. The best-qualified people get the jobs.
60. When interviewers say you're overqualified, they really mean you're too old.
61. There's no such thing as job security.

Myth #39

Some job interviews are a waste of time.

Reality

There is a two-fold reality here:

1. Every interview is a rehearsal for the one that results in a job offer.
2. An interview offers an opportunity to learn more about the company and industry, even if you're not excited about that particular job.

Discussion

You can never practice interviewing enough. Even if in retrospect you feel you weren't qualified for the job, a good interview could lead to other opportunities within the company. Be positive and be glad you had the chance to meet a representative of the organization. At the very least, it's good practice.

Example: Andrew Holmes had three interviews lined up by the second week of his job search. It had been 6 years since he'd gone through the interview process, so he felt somewhat nervous about what lay ahead.

He made it through the first interview, in his words, "okay." It had been what Holmes described as "your basic interview." But, when Holmes went to a second interview, he realized he felt more confident and relaxed. By the third interview, he came home smiling. As it turned out, he got a job offer from the second company, which happened to be his first choice. He commented later, however, about how much more comfortable he'd felt in each successive interview.

Some job seekers are so selective about with whom they speak that they unknowingly reject potential opportunities.

Examples: Eva Taglienta said, "I was too picky about opportunities. Some jobs weren't exactly what I wanted. It wasn't until later that I realized there was hidden potential in some of the opportunities to interview that I passed up." Mary Lou Yoder had a similar experience: "I didn't realize that every chance to interview, whether or not I was excited about the job, was a foot in the door. I blew it."

Both women learned from their mistaken belief that some interviews are a waste of time.

On the other hand, keeping an open mind and having the right attitude with regard to interviewing opportunities can reap rewards.

Example: Ralph Timmons had decided to make a major change in his life and career. He understood the potential consequences of his decision and decided to consider all possibilities. Timmons applied everywhere he felt there was even a remote chance of employment. His break came when he went on an interview for a particular job, but impressed the interviewer so favorably that he became a candidate for three higher level openings as well.

As you prepare for each job interview consider this:

- Prepare for each interview as if it were for your dream job.
- Even if you're unemployed, act as if you're employed. Never give the impression that you're desperate.
- Look and act like a winner.

The old saying, "practice makes perfect," can apply to some degree to interviews. Since each interviewer will have his or her personal approach, each interview will be somewhat different. On the other hand, certain basics pertain to the interview process and certain questions will come up over and over again.

Look at each interview as an opportunity to "practice toward perfection."

Myth #40

You probably won't be asked to participate in a video conference interview.

Reality

Employment interviewing is a relatively new application of video conference technology, but employers do use it and you need to be prepared.

Discussion

If you're invited to participate in a video conference job interview consider the following advice from Dr. Karl Magnusen of the College of Business Administration at Florida International University.

Do:
- Wear solid colors; light blue shirts or blouses look better on screen than white.
- Begin the interview with a smile, because you won't be able to shake hands.

- Keep in mind there will be a half-second delay in transmission. As a result, participants must listen more carefully.
- Behave as though you're in a normal office interview. Remember, the other party can hear everything unless you use a mute feature. Make certain that there will be no potential distractions from a child, friend, spouse, etc. during the interview.
- Check time zone differences when scheduling.

Don't:
- Be late.
- Wear clothing, scarves, or ties with busy patterns; they're distracting. Similarly, avoid jewelry or cuff links that may clink next to the microphone.
- Make too many movements. While normal movement is fine, excessive gesturing will wash out on the screen, because data transmission is not sophisticated enough.
- Forget that you're talking to a real person like yourself. Concentrate on the interview, not the technology.
- Neglect to thank the other person at the end of the interview.

Except for the fact that your interviewer isn't in the room with you, the interview will be like any other in many respects. You'll want to prepare to answer the interviewer's questions and to ask questions of your own. The interviewer will still evaluate you on how you conduct yourself in the interview. In addition to the "do" and "don't" items, follow the same guidelines that you use for any interview.

Examples: Glen Christiansen, a job seeker, shared the following experience: "I was asked to participate in a video conference interview. I've always been kind of camera shy so it took a lot for me to convince myself to follow through, but it wasn't as bad as I had anticipated. I concentrated on what I was saying and pretended it was just like a regular interview in someone's office. I didn't get the job, but I was called in for a personal interview that went well. My advice would be to stay calm and try to forget you're on television."

Debbie Hart added this advice: "As a human resource generalist, part of my responsibility is to set up video conference interviews with candidates. Our company uses them because they're efficient and cost-effective. I find that people who look nervous are no different in person. Candidates who have confidence and are able to sell themselves in a face-to-face interview are successful in front of a camera as well. My suggestion to anyone who's asked to participate in a video conference job interview is to prepare just as you would for an on-site visit with an employer and you will be fine."

Myth #41

The interview begins when you meet the interviewer.

Reality

For a face-to-face, office interview, the interview begins when you set foot on company property.

Discussion

Be prepared. You never know who's watching. There's always the possibility that someone's observing you as you park your car, walk to the door, and sit down in the lobby. Example: The president of a well-known company said he refuses to hire candidates who look like they lack energy as they walk from the parking lot to his office.

Once you arrive, be friendly; but don't flirt with the receptionist or crack jokes. Don't talk in a loud voice or pace nervously. Look interested in the surroundings and read any available company literature. Some organizations have scrapbooks and photos of company events in the reception area. Reviewing these materials will help you get a better feel for the business.

If you think your hair is wind-blown, check a mirror (discreetly of course) or visit the restroom so you can take one last look at yourself before the interviewer sees you. This also gives you a last chance to check your clothing for any turned collars, untrimmed threads, exposed tags, etc.

Natalie Barnes, quality control manager in the high-tech industry, says that many candidates don't pay attention to detail. People who interview with her must pass her office window before entering the building. "I see people doing some embarrassing things thinking no one is looking. They don't realize that the tinted glass in my office allows me to see them and form an impression before we meet face to face. Even energy that's projected in the way someone walks could be an influencing factor." Her best advice is, "Be ready at all times once you arrive at the place of your interview or you could lose an opportunity and never know why."

Example: Shirley Grimm provides an example of what not to do. She arrived early for an interview for a position as a sales representative. The reception area was part of the senior secretary's office. When the secretary asked for her resume (in accordance with the manager's instructions for all interviews; he liked to see what the candidate would bring), Grimm argued with her. She refused to give it to the secretary and said she would take it in with her. Instead of advising her manager via the intercom that the candidate had arrived, the secretary delivered the message personally and conveyed Grimm's remarks about the resume.

Grimm also asked the secretary to make "a few copies" of the resume for her, "...since you already have a copy." She interrupted the secretary's work several times with questions, trying to obtain information about how many other candidates they had interviewed, what kind of person was the hiring manager, whether she [Grimm] looked okay, etc. She also asked to use the office telephone to make a brief personal call that wasn't brief. Ms. Grimm apparently thought the secretary was deaf because she made inappropriate comments on the telephone about her personal job situation. The secretary remained gracious and calm throughout the entire situation, but was relieved when the candidate finally went in for her interview.

The secretary and her manager had worked together for 5 years and were a close team. He valued her opinion, and knew she was always honest in her answers. His first question to the secretary after Grimm left was, "Well, what did you think of her?"

What do you think the secretary said?

Myth #42

Employers are more interested in what you have to say than what you wear to the interview.

Reality

Employers make judgments about you from the moment they see you. A professional appearance can give you an edge.

Discussion

Dress conservatively, even for interviews with companies where casual dress is the daily norm. You do not want to appear to be a trendsetter.

For men:
Wear:

- A good quality navy, gray, or charcoal-colored suit.
- A solid white, starched shirt.
- A contemporary tie with respect to color, width, and pattern.
- Lace-up or wing-tip leather shoes. Be sure they're polished.

- Socks in a color that matches your trousers and that will cover your legs if you cross them.
- A leather belt that matches the color of your shoes.

Also:

- Hair and nails should be trimmed and cleaned.
- A clean-shaven look is best.
- Watches should be gold, stainless steel, or a good quality imitation. Sport watches are unacceptable.
- Avoid earrings, bracelets, necklaces, and rings (other than a wedding band).

For women:
Wear:

- A suit, or jacket and color-coordinated skirt. The skirt should be no shorter than just above the knee. If you're short, breaking colors (different color top and bottom) will make you look shorter.
- Conservative makeup meant to enhance your features, not cover them with a mask.
- No more than one ring on each hand (except for a wedding set).
- Quality and conservative jewelry (earrings, pin, necklace).
- Polished leather pumps with one- to two-inch heels.
- Neutral-colored hosiery.

Also:

- Keep nails well manicured. Chipped polish draws attention to your hands.
- Carry a briefcase or a handbag, but not both.
- Only men can get away without shaving their legs.
- Go light on perfume. A fragrance you find pleasant may smell like bug spray to others, or the interviewer may have an allergy to some fragrances.

Buy the best quality clothing you can afford, and make sure it fits properly. Your clothing will look best when pressed and clean. If you don't know what colors suit you, find out by having a color analysis.

Example: Claude Stephens successfully completed a drafting course with high marks. The school arranged an interview with a well-known firm and advised him to dress conservatively. Stephens, who preferred extremely casual dress for every occasion, dressed to please himself. He had the attitude that if he could do the job, what he wore shouldn't matter as long as it was neat and clean. It did matter, and Stephens didn't get the job for which he was actually very well-qualified.

As you prepare for the interview, keep in mind that you want them to remember you for what you said, not what you wore.

Myth #43

When asked what kind of job you're looking for, it's acceptable to say, "Anything that's available."

Reality

Employers don't like to waste time with candidates who are "open to anything" or appear unfocused.

Discussion

In most cases you'll be applying for a specific job. However, there may be times when you're cold-calling or involved in an informational interview. In both situations, you need to be specific about your job goal.

Employers are interested in three things:

1. Are you qualified to do the job?
2. Are you interested in performing the job duties they have in mind?
3. Are you a team player who will fit in with the rest of the employees?

Whether your first meeting is by telephone or during a personal interview, you'll want to be ready with a 30-second overview of who you are and what you're looking for. A typical dialogue might sound like this, once you've exchanged the usual salutations and introductions:

Employer: "Let's begin with you telling me about what kind of job you're looking for."

Candidate: "Okay. I'm seeking a position as a strategic planner. I've worked in the field for the past 5 years. In my last job at XYZ Corporation, I was responsible for regional strategy, planning, and forecasting. Last year I developed a strategic business plan that supported a 2.5-million-dollar capital improvement project. I also analyzed a regional sales trend model in order to forecast operating revenue for a 50-million-dollar region."

In contrast to the example above, T.J. Sinclair provides an example of what *not* to say.

Example: Sinclair had worked for a health care referral service, but was terminated for excessive absenteeism. He started his job search feeling down and ready to accept anything that paid enough to put food on the table.

When asked what he was looking for, his usual reply was, "What have you got that pays a decent wage?" Employers were unimpressed with his response. It took him longer than it should have to find another position comparable to the one he had previously.

Employers expect you to know what you're looking for in a job. Don't expect them to serve up a smorgasbord of jobs for you to choose from. They have neither the time nor the inclination. "Anything that's available," may make an impression, but it probably won't be the one you intended.

Myth #44

Your goal in the interview is to share as much as you can about yourself.

Reality

Most candidates talk too much during the interview.

Discussion

You'll want to sell yourself and what you have to offer during the interview, without revealing too much and potentially eliminating yourself from consideration. Just answer the questions. If the interviewer wants to know more about you, he or she will ask another question.

Here are some ideas for helping you keep your interview on target:

1. Understand that although you're there to sell yourself, a good sales-person also knows how to listen. Good listening skills enable you to answer the question the interviewer asked, rather than the question you expected.
2. Be prepared to respond to the following in two minutes or less: "Tell me about yourself." It's probably a good idea to write down this information before the interview and be able to articulate it, so you won't ramble.

3. Know how you can contribute to the success of the organization and be able to explain the "how" if asked.

4. Anticipate questions. Although interviewers often ask similar questions, you need to consider in advance what particular questions an interviewer might ask with regard to a specific job. (If an interviewer surprises you with a totally unanticipated question, take a few moments to collect your thoughts before you answer. Blurting out what comes to mind first could cost you the job.)

5. Learn as much as you can from the interviewer about the organization, position, and job requirements. Then, be prepared to tell him or her what makes you uniquely qualified for the job.

6. Mirror the interviewer's body language and speech. Listen to his or her speech patterns (speed, tone of speech). Does the interviewer tend to use "I see," "I hear," or "I feel" in the conversation? If you present yourself in a format that comes naturally to the interviewer, you'll make a better impression.

7. Never apologize for what you don't have or point out your weaknesses or disabilities (see Myth #46). Your job is to sell your strengths and abilities. Make positive statements with your answers.

8. Your share of the conversation with an interviewer should be 50 percent. If there are two interviewers, your share is 30 percent.

Example: Helen Overton went to the job interview with confidence. The position was one in which she had extensive experience and she had taken time to gather information about the corporation. She dressed professionally, arrived on time for the interview, greeted the interviewer appropriately, and remembered to smile. Unfortunately, Overton made a major mistake—she took charge of the interview. In her efforts to sell herself, she interrupted the interviewer's questions to give her replies, talked at length about unnecessary details, and told the interviewer how she would "straighten out" things if she had the job. She mistook the interviewer's willingness to let her talk as interest in what she had to say, when in reality it was a case of "giving her enough rope to hang herself," which she did. Despite her qualifications, Overton didn't get the job offer. She actually talked herself out of a job.

As you prepare for the interview, plan to leave a lasting impression. Leave them thinking you're a qualified, intelligent, and personable candidate—a perfect fit for the job. Don't make them sorry they met you because you didn't know when to talk and when to listen.

Myth #45

An effective way to let the interviewer know you're relaxed is by telling a joke.

Reality

A sense of humor is a desirable trait, but too much or inappropriate humor can ruin your chances for a job offer.

Discussion

When you've prepared for the interview you'll feel confident in yourself and what you have to offer and naturally appear more relaxed.

The interviewer will know you're relaxed because you have:

1. A firm handshake.
2. Good eye contact.
3. A smile that says, "I'm happy to be here."
4. An "I can do it" attitude.

Focus on understanding rather than being understood. This will also help you get over nervousness. Candidates who try to fill the silence with jokes or nervous laughter only hurt their chances for getting the job offer.

Examples: Job hunter Tim Bond shared this advice: "I'm a pretty funny guy, but when I got a little crazy in the interview it was a big mistake. The interviewer encouraged me and I kept telling jokes and funny stories. My behavior bordered on flirtatious. I was attracted to her and I was dumb enough to believe that she was also attracted to me so I continued my outrageous antics. I learned later the reason I didn't get the job was because she didn't think I was qualified. That's probably because I spent most of my time during the interview trying to impress her with my humor. I believe I was very qualified but never took the time to tell the interviewer what my strengths were in relationship to the job. To add insult to injury, I found out she was married."

Tina Ann Rubin is another example of how an interviewer might view humor as inappropriate. She was a stand-up comic in New York City who decided to return to a more traditional career in computers. A funny lady, at the end of the interview she told the male interviewer a dirty joke that she planned to use in her next act. He laughed but wasn't impressed. She didn't get the job.

A good rule to follow: If in doubt, leave it out.

Myth #46

When asked about your weaknesses, answer honestly.

Reality

Never make a negative statement about yourself. Accentuate the positive.

Discussion

Some interviewers may simply say, "Tell me about what you consider to be your weaknesses." Others may use probing questions such as the following to try to determine your weaknesses:

- Did you do your best in school? If not, why not?
- Have you ever cheated or been tempted to cheat on a test? Tell me about it.
- Did you ever fail in a class? If yes, what was the reason?
- Describe a time when you encountered obstacles in your last job that you were unable to overcome. What happened?
- How did you handle your biggest career disappointment?
- Tell me about a time when you had to lower your standards.

- Give me an example of a time when you were put on the spot.
- What do you think could potentially interfere with your effectiveness as a leader?
- What do you enjoy least about being a leader?
- Tell me about a time when you caused a breakdown in communication at work.
- Tell me about a time when your boss criticized your work.
- How would you discuss your job dissatisfaction with your current or last boss?
- What would you say to an employee who is frequently late for work?
- In what kind of work environment are you uncomfortable?
- When you don't meet your goals, how do you handle it?
- What kind of customers upset you?
- How do you handle rejection?
- What kinds of decisions are the most difficult for you to make?
- We all make errors in judgment from time to time. Tell me about the last time you made an error in judgment.
- What is the worst decision you have made in a previous job? Why did you make it? How did you correct the problem?
- Tell me about a time when many people were counting on you and you failed to solve the problem.
- Tell me about a recurring problem that you would have liked to have solved in your current or last job but haven't yet.
- Tell me about a bad decision you made while under a lot of pressure.

There are several ways to handle questions about your weaknesses. The goal is to answer the question, but in a way that accentuates the positive. You don't want to create a negative impression about your work skills or ability to fit in with the company.

One way you could respond when asked a general question about your weaknesses is to mention a weakness that's not related to the particular job you're seeking. Or, you can discuss a weakness that's already apparent from the information on your resume, such as your grade point average. Even so, you will want to end your comments with a positive statement.

Another tactic is to present a weakness, but then present a positive side. Instead of, "I'm too time conscious," try, "Some people may consider me too time conscious, but most people appreciate the fact that I don't waste time and always complete my projects before they are due."

Try to present a personal weakness as a professional strength. Example: "Although I have good people skills, I am able to work well on teams or alone, and have excellent reasoning abilities. I believe a weakness would be that I could use more experience in the field." This answer allows you to say something positive about yourself, while admitting to a fairly common weakness. (Everyone can benefit from experience.) You'll also earn points for being honest.

Don't use a flippant answer such as, "I don't have any weaknesses," or make a joke to answer this question. The interviewer asked it as a serious question. Such a response could indicate to the interviewer that you aren't taking the situation seriously. If the interviewer accepts your answer as a serious response, he or she will probably believe you have little insight into yourself.

Also, keep in mind that what's perceived as a weakness in one job may not count as a weakness for another position. Not every job requires that you be a managerial candidate.

Although an interviewer may use probing questions in an effort to determine your weaknesses, the opposite may actually occur. Probing questions can also give you the opportunity to share your strengths. For example, if the interviewer asks, "What do you enjoy least about being a leader?," you could reply: "I enjoy working in a leadership position and haven't encountered any major difficulties. If I had to name one thing that I wouldn't enjoy it would be to see employees who refuse to live up to their potential despite my encouragement and willingness to work with them. I prefer to see all of the people I supervise fulfill their personal potential."

Questions about your weaknesses, whether direct or probing, are something you'll definitely want to think through and prepare an answer for ahead of time because most interviewers will use some form of the question. If you've given time and consideration to your answers beforehand, however, you should be able to turn them into an opportunity to offset any weakness with a point of strength.

Myth #47

Never ask questions in the interview; that's the interviewer's job.

Reality

Be ready with good questions. At the end of the interview, you will be asked if you have questions.

Discussion

The type of questions you ask will depend upon what stage you've reached in the interview process. The questions you ask at the end of a first interview could vary greatly from what you'd want to ask at the end of a third or fourth interview.

What you ask and at what stage is up to you. The answers to your questions are important and will help you decide whether or not to accept the position.

Some questions you might want to ask are provided here.

Questions about the organization:
- What position does the organization have in the industry? Is it the market leader, in the middle, or does it have to market through other avenues? (You should have made a concerted effort to obtain this kind of information prior to the interview through your research of the company. The form of your question could indicate whether you made such an attempt.)
- How does the business market its products or services to clients or customers?
- Does the company have a policy of promotion from within or does it generally look outside for talent?

Questions about job duties and responsibilities:
- What kind of authority does the position have? What decisions could I make without getting higher management or committee approval?
- Can you describe a typical day for me?
- Does this position involve a lot of travel?

Questions about the department:
- What is the current status of the department? What are its strengths and weaknesses?
- What is different about this department that sets it apart from other similar departments in the organization?
- What is the rate of turnover in this department?

Questions about compensation and benefits (don't get into this unless you have a job offer):
- What part of the compensation plan is tied to performance?
- What kinds of benefits are available in terms of medical, dental, life insurance, etc.?
- Would I be asked to sign an employment contract? If so, what are the terms?

Questions about relocation (if you have to move):
- What moving expenses does the company pay?
- Will the company pay for one or more trips for my spouse to see the community and look for housing?

- If the move is delayed for any reason, will the company provide transportation for me to visit my family regularly?

These sample questions are a good place to start, provided of course you're not expected to know the answers as a result of your company research. You don't want to give the impression you don't know anything about the organization that's interviewing you, or ask a question that you should know the answer to.

In addition, there are questions you can ask to help you determine in a diplomatic way whether someone higher than the interviewer will make the final choice. For example:

- Who would supervise the person in this position?
- Is there someone else who will be involved in the final hiring decision for this job?

Another question you may ask the interviewer is how he or she would rate your qualifications for the job. The reply should help you learn whether or not you're in the running for the job. It may also give you information about a point the interviewer saw as a problem, but wouldn't have discussed with you otherwise. This then gives you the opportunity to explain, defend, or clarify the point of concern. If there's concern over a perceived weakness, you could assure the interviewer of your willingness to work to overcome it.

The interviewer may, of course, tell you she's not ready to give you feedback at that time. Even this reply can set the stage for you to briefly summarize the strengths you could bring to the job.

There's one question that candidates often overlook: Asking for the job. Ask in a pleasant and confident manner, and you won't appear overly aggressive. This doesn't mean you should say, "May I have the job?" but you do let the person know that you feel you're a good candidate and why, that you're very interested in the job, and that you hope you will be the candidate selected to fill the position.

Asking questions may be difficult for some candidates, either because of lack of interview experience or because they have difficulty feeling it's appropriate. However, the interviewer expects you to have questions. A candidate who has no questions might cause as much concern in the interviewer as the candidate who goes overboard and asks too many questions.

Before you leave the interviewer's office, ask about the next step in the selection process. When can you expect to hear from the interviewer? When do they expect to make a decision? By what date do they need to fill the position? Often people neglect to get this information. Then they wait and wonder whether they haven't heard because they weren't selected or because the employer hasn't finished the interviews. (If no one contacts you by the date given, don't hesitate to follow up by phone. It demonstrates a sincere interest in the job and shows that you can take initiative.)

*   *   *

Take notes during the interview, but ask permission to do so. The interviewer won't refuse your request. Have a pen and pad ready to jot down important items. This will help you make a good impression and also provides the information you need for your interview summary later and for the follow up letter.

Myth #48

Employers are willing to sacrifice technical expertise to attract candidates.

Reality

You still have to know your stuff.

Discussion

As desperate as some employers are to find good help, most want employees who at least meet their minimum job requirements. Most interviewers may not have an in-depth knowledge of every job in the organization, but they understand enough to know that a certain level of technical expertise is mandatory. Don't try to fake it and convince employers that you're someone you're not. This tactic seldom works. Even if it did work, the fact that you don't know what you claimed would soon become apparent once you're on the job.

Instead, as you prepare for the interview:

Know what you want to say about your skills and abilities:
- Give examples of things you've done in previous jobs that pertain to the job for which you're applying.

- Mention major responsibilities of your previous/current job.
- Mention a significant project that you completed.
- Highlight independent or team work as applicable.
- Tell how you encountered and overcame an obstacle.
- Mention your leadership skills.

Relate what you have to offer to the job requirements:
- If they're looking for a sales representative with 5 years of outside sales experience and you have what they need, tell them how well you did and how your employer benefited.
- If you don't have exactly what they're seeking, emphasize what you do have. Maybe you have 2 years of volunteer work in the field plus 3 years of paid experience. Tell them.
- Mention ways your previous job prepared you for greater responsibilities.

It's okay to "toot your own horn," but don't overdo it. Sometimes it's how you present the information. For example, "I felt proud of my staff and our team accomplishments and the fact that my team members felt free to come to me when they had a problem," sounds better than, "I was the best manager in the company."

If you appear to lack the necessary degree of technical expertise, you must demonstrate to the employer how your transferable skills can make up for that deficiency. You may also point out that moving from one industry to another enables you to bring a fresh perspective to the job.

Often people who have the skills fail to identify them. The terminology may differ from industry to industry, but the language is basically the same. For example, one candidate discovered that what his field of work called "client management" translated into "product management" in another field.

Myth #49

Employers know better than to ask inappropriate or illegal questions.

Reality

Although inappropriate and illegal questions reflect badly on the interviewer and his or her employer, it's still a problem even in today's lawsuit-happy society.

Discussion

An interviewer may ask you an illegal question for a number of reasons:

1. Ignorance of the law regarding certain questions.
2. Disregard of the law regarding certain questions (to see if they can get the information).
3. To see how you handle such questions. (In other words, do you give them the information or do you stand up for your rights?)

Even questions that aren't illegal may be in poor taste. Examples include:

- Have you considered losing weight?
- Have you ever cheated on your wife/husband?

- What would you say if I told you to take off your clothing?
- What do you think about same-sex marriages?

You have three choices when asked a question you'd rather not answer:

1. Forget your civil rights and answer.
2. Answer without answering.
3. Refuse to answer.

Forget your civil rights and answer. If you choose to answer an illegal or inappropriate question, you're providing non-job-related information. The "wrong" answer could cost you a job offer. Also, the fact that you were willing to answer an illegal or inappropriate question could reflect poorly on you as a candidate, depending upon the interviewer's motives in asking the question. He or she may be testing your resoluteness. Answering does not guarantee you'll get the job.

Answer without answering. In this instance, examine the intent of the questioner and then answer in response to that intent. Sometimes interviewers have legitimate concerns, but ask the question the wrong way.

For example, if asked:

"What will your spouse think about you traveling?"
The interviewer has concern about whether there'll be a problem from a husband/wife if you travel. He doesn't want to hire you and then hear, "My wife/husband doesn't like me to be out of town."

You could respond with,

"Travel has never been a problem."

Or, if asked:

"Who will take care of your children when you're working?"
The interviewer has concern about absenteeism from the job due to needs of small children.

You could say,

"I never let personal commitments interfere with my professional life."

Or, if asked:

> "How old are you?"

The interviewer should know better than this, but may have concern about whether age will affect job performance.

You could say,

> "My age has never been a factor in my job performance."

In these three examples, your response addresses what you perceive as the interviewer's concern, but does not give personal information.

Refuse to answer. You could say, "I'm sorry, but I consider that question an invasion of my privacy and I will not answer it." When you refuse to answer a question, you're well within your rights. However, you run the risk of sounding uncooperative or confrontational, not someone an employer would be interested in hiring.

The goal here is to refuse to answer but to do it as tactfully as possible. Your demeanor and facial expression while you answer is also important. Be gracious but firm. Example:

> "I'm sure you didn't mean to ask me an illegal question. Could we go on to the next question?"

Or,

> "I assume you didn't realize you've just asked me an illegal question. Why don't we just go on to the next question?"

The interviewer may feel embarrassed or angry when you point out his or her mistake, or he or she may like the fact that you didn't hesitate to refuse to answer. If you decide to use this response, all you can do is state it in a non-confrontational tone while keeping a pleasant expression on your face.

Another strategy is to respond with an answer that has nothing to do with the question. For example: The interviewer asks you whether you've ever had an affair. Your response: *"I think my years of experience operating a computer would serve me very well on this job."* If the interviewer asks a second time, give the same answer to clarify that you didn't misunderstand the question the first time.

If you're not sure which questions are illegal, see Appendix D. Many interviewers ask such questions without realizing what they've done, or ask because of inexperience. Others may deliberately ask such questions. Either way, your best defense is to be aware of the possibility of such questions and be prepared with how you will respond.

Myth #50

It's best to share your salary expectations when you meet the interviewer to avoid misunderstandings later.

Reality

Never bring up pay before a prospective employer mentions it. It's best to avoid it entirely during the first interview if possible.

Discussion

Asking salary-related questions early in the interview process shows the employer your focus is more on what you can get rather than what you can give. In addition, by bringing up the matter prematurely, you may name a figure that's below what the company would have offered.

Other factors to consider before beginning the discussion of money is whether there's opportunity for advancement, the possibility of lay-off (recent or expected), etc. For example, you might accept a slightly lower than desired salary for a position that offers good growth potential.

This doesn't mean you don't have salary expectations at the beginning. You need to know what you consider your market value before the money question arises. You'll need to know the minimum you're willing to work for if the job you want the most happens to pay the least. You'll need to consider whether other benefits such as more vacation time, personal days, compensatory time, etc., are as or more important to you than a certain dollar amount. Knowing this in advance prepares you for the discussion of compensation at the appropriate time.

Another side of the question is, "What do you do if the interviewer brings up money early in the interview?" Ask yourself what motive the interviewer could have for doing this. Is he or she truly concerned about whether you're affordable? Not likely. Maybe it's a question intended primarily to gauge your response.

Consider the effect of these responses to the interviewer's question, *"What kind of salary did you have in mind?"*

Response A: "I would need a minimum of $30,000 yearly plus a company car, and would expect a 5 percent bonus at the end of the first year."
The interviewer hears: *"Compensation is very important to me."* In addition, the company had planned to pay up to $40,000, plus a 10 percent bonus, and all account executives get a company car. The candidate has set a lower salary for himself than the company may have offered.

Response B: "I was looking at a range between $30,000 and $40,000 plus company benefits depending upon the job responsibilities."
The interviewer hears: *"Compensation is important to me, but I'm not sure how much I'm worth."* The candidate has set a definite range limit. This could:

    (a) Eliminate him or her from consideration if it's too much, or

    (b) Cause the company to offer the candidate less if it's too low.

Response C: "Well, Mr. Brown, I'm probably like most other people in that I want to make as much money as I can. But I'm also very interested in the challenges involved in this position. From what we've discussed so far, I believe I'm capable of meeting the job demands. What is the starting salary for someone in this position?"
The interviewer hears: *"I'm interested, but you're going to have to start the bidding."* The candidate has left room for both parties to negotiate and hasn't limited him/herself to a set figure.

The initial interview is the time to focus on convincing the employer you're the right person for the job, while also deciding if you have an interest in accepting the position. Once the company decides they want to hire you, you're in a position to negotiate compensation and benefits.

Myth #51

There's no way to prepare for pre-employment tests.

Reality

Although you can't study for these tests, you can mentally prepare to do the best you can and take that attitude with you when taking tests.

Discussion

"There's nothing to fear." Those words have cost candidates jobs. Why? Because they didn't take the tests seriously. If the prospective employer asks you to take a career assessment, intelligence, abilities, or psychological test, give it your best effort, including answering truthfully.

Example: Consider the case of a computer programmer who was a poor test taker. He "studied" the night before and the next day answered the way he thought he should answer. He didn't know the test had a built-in indicator that could detect deception. He lost the job to another candidate because the employer knew he had lied.

One tip to keep in mind, however, is to avoid extremes when you answer. If you have a choice of "never," "rarely," "sometimes," or "always", choose the less dogmatic answer.

Try to view taking the test as an experience that can help you in the future even if you don't get the job this time.

Example: A recruiter phoned Ann Raporpart, a sales manager, about an exciting opportunity. However, the company required candidates to take a battery of psychological and intelligence tests.

"I was very concerned when he told me about the tests," said Raporpart. "I'm not a good test-taker. I had no choice, but it wasn't as bad as I had anticipated. Although I didn't get the job, the experience prepared me for the job I eventually got for which I was also tested. I felt much more at ease and prepared the second time. I quickly answered each true/false question and then put the entire experience out of my mind. I was pleasantly surprised when the recruiter called to tell me the company wanted to make me a job offer. I've worked there for 6 years and have used pre-employment tests to help me with hiring decisions. The results are quite accurate in predicting future job performance, so do your best if asked to take a test."

Many pre-employment exercises will take only about an hour to finish. Some may be more involved. The intent is not to be unfriendly, but to help the prospective employer evaluate you as a candidate and how well you'll fit into a particular position within the company.

If you've never had to take a test as part of the interview process, that doesn't mean it will never happen. Tests of all types are used in business today—not only in hiring new employees, but in evaluating candidates for promotion.

Tests help measure personality, values, and preferences. However, tests are only part of the process. The personal interview is still the best way to win a job.

Myth #52

Follow up after an interview may give the impression you're desperate for a job.

Reality

Failure to follow up is one of the biggest mistakes you can make.

Discussion

Employers not only notice when you take the initiative to follow up, but they expect it. Consider making a telephone call to reinforce your interest in the position as well as thank the interviewer again for taking the time to meet with you. At the very least, follow up with a thank you letter. This allows you to confirm your continued interest after the interview and remind the interviewer why you stood out from the crowd. It also gives you another chance to reinforce a decision to hire you. A customized thank you letter is another key tool in your job search.

For example, Tom Thomas, an engineering manager who's hired hundreds of people during his career, had this to say about follow up: "It always surprises me when candidates don't know enough to send a thank you letter or note. I guess they don't understand that I evaluate everything about them, from their ability to convince me they're right for the job to their manners. I also expect candidates to follow up with a call, especially if they have questions or want to re-emphasize their interest in the job."

Dean Williams, M.D., had similar feedback: "When I spend time interviewing, I expect candidates to show interest with a follow up thank you by mail and/or telephone. Even if I'm unable to take the call, my secretary will give me the message. Candidates who don't know enough to follow up won't survive working in my busy office."

What happens when you follow up and don't get the job offer? Follow up again. Consider the case of the candidate who thought the interview had gone well, sent a thank you/follow up letter, but then learned he didn't get the job. He promptly sent another letter in which he expressed his regret at not being selected and his hope that the company would consider him for future openings. He closed with his thanks for their time and interest, and said he looked forward to hearing from them.

The letter so impressed the interviewer that he called the candidate and assured him that even though they had no job openings, he would definitely consider him for a future opportunity.

When you follow up, you expand your employment opportunities. You're also investing time in creating future possibilities. Sometimes a candidate impresses the employer favorably, but isn't an exact fit for the position they're filling. The candidate might be right for a future position, but needs to ensure that the interviewer remembers him or her.

Sometimes the candidate has everything—qualifications, abilities, fit—but the competition is very keen. There may be three strong and almost equal finalists, but only one can get the job. The follow up letter may make the difference when the company makes the final decision.

The follow up letter is an integral part of the interview process. The prospective employer expects one, it offers candidates one more chance to sell themselves to the employer and keep their options alive, and it may tip the scales in the candidate's favor when he or she is compared to the competition.

Myth #53

Expressing gratitude in a thank you letter is enough.

Reality

Saying "thank you" in a letter is important. However, it's not enough by itself. The follow up letter must say much more if you want it to be effective.

Discussion

A thank you letter is another opportunity for you to sell yourself to the prospective employer, to reinforce your skills, work experience, and the fact that you want the job and are a perfect fit. Send a different thank you letter to every person who interviewed you, even if you met with 15 people. Employers often remember the little things long after you've left.

The three main sections of a thank you letter are:

1. The opener (pleasure meeting you)
2. Reinforcement (feel well-suited for job)
   or
   Recovery (although lacking in one area, other skills compensate)
3. Close (your chance to tell them again that you could make a contribution to the company and want the job)

Always use crisp, clean paper, and follow the other guidelines with regard to paper and printing quality for cover letters (see Myths #18–21). In particular, as with cover letters, thank you letters should not be handwritten. And use your own stationery, not your employer's.

The experts agree that if you follow these guidelines when sending a thank you letter it can improve your chances for a job offer:

- Keep your letter brief—one page is sufficient.
- Be friendly—let the tone of the letter match the tone of the interview. If the interview was casual and relaxed, write your letter in the same manner. If the interview was formal, follow the same style in your letter, but be friendly.
- Reinforce anything that's important, such as relevant skills and experience that are of interest to the company.
- If you've thought of something you should have covered during the interview but didn't, include it in the letter.
- Close with a positive statement, such as, "I would enjoy working with you and look forward to hearing from you soon."

In surveying human resources managers nationwide, I found that most of them aren't getting the expected thank you letters from candidates. They verified the fact that a well-written "thank you" could be a deciding factor in determining who among the finalists gets the job.

Myth #54

Most companies don't check references.

Reality

Reference checking is an important step used by employers to gather information on prospective candidates.

Discussion

Although checking references today is a great deal more structured and liability-conscious procedure than years ago, a recent survey by the Society for Human Resource Management indicated that employers still check references.

Therefore, you need to select your references carefully. Prospective employers will want to speak with people who are familiar with your work (see Myth #55). You'll also want to notify references before someone contacts them, and discuss with them the job you're seeking. References who are surprised by a phone call may not be prepared to help sell you to a future employer.

Examples: Eleanor Parker-Jones didn't prepare her references for the calls they received. As a result, none were effective salespeople for her candidacy.

As she put it, "If I had to do it over again I would have contacted my references after I knew the company was going to call them. I would have told them what I wanted them to emphasize and how important the job was to me. I took for granted that they would know what to do, but I was wrong."

Al Givens interviewed for a job, and then notified his references. But he failed to explain to them exactly what he would be doing if hired. The references were confused when contacted because Givens was making a career change that his references knew nothing about. Givens explained: "I've had several jobs in different fields over the last 15 years. I was a social worker, head chef, boy scout camp director, and computer operator. I decided to try working as a small machine repairman, something I did as a hobby, but that most people didn't know I enjoyed. My references were confused when called by prospective employers. My lack of preparation in explaining to my references what kind of job I was interviewing for was a mistake."

Frank Reuter was successful because he coached his references: "I left nothing to chance. I wanted to be sure each person who agreed to be a reference knew that I was qualified for the job. I also provided each with a copy of my resume. I let them know how much I wanted the position."

Reuter, unlike Parker-Jones and Givens, did his homework. He got the job. He thanked his references, and continues to keep in touch with them because he knows he may need their help again.

Make sure the people you list as references understand the importance of agreeing to be a reference. If you're in doubt about using someone as a reference, don't use that person. Even a neutral reference can cost you an opportunity.

Follow these guidelines when choosing references:

- Select people you can trust.
- Ask permission to use them as a reference.
- Ask them what they're going to say.
- Suggest they speak about a project you worked on jointly or mention your outstanding traits.

In addition, employers know you're going to include only those people who will say positive things about you, so some may ask your references if they can suggest someone else to speak to about you. Discuss this possibility beforehand with your references and agree on whom they will suggest to the caller if this happens.

Avoid the temptation to use someone you hardly know as a reference just because they're prestigious. They won't know enough about you to really give an impressive reference. In addition, the interviewer will readily recognize that you attempted to use the influence of a well-known name rather than someone who could discuss your qualifications as an employee. They'll wonder why you felt it necessary to do this.

A good gauge for how well you know someone is whether you're able to be very open with them about the importance of their reference. If not, don't use them as a reference.

Remember, your references are an important sales tool in obtaining your next position.

Myth #55

Personal references are as useful as work-related references.

Reality

Prospective employers want to speak to people who are familiar with your work. Friends and acquaintances aren't good enough as references unless you've worked for them.

Discussion

If you're a recent graduate with limited work experience, you'll want to list as references your professors, volunteer work supervisors, etc., in addition to whatever employment references you have.

If you've been working for several years, your references should include your current or former supervisors, subordinates, and co-workers. These people know your work habits best and can provide information concerning your qualifications and ability to perform the job. The caller will ask about your professional strengths and weaknesses, how you get along with others, how you respond to criticisms, etc. Only people who've worked with you can answer these questions.

Companies conduct reference checks to confirm what the prospective employer believes to be true about you. References must know enough about you and the job you're applying for to speak on your behalf. Although friends or acquaintances may be able to vouch for your wonderful personality, they won't be able to tell a prospective employer how well you hold up under pressure on the job, whether you're a team player at work, how well you managed an important project, etc. These are the things about which the employer is trying to gather information.

Myth #56

If you didn't get along with your former boss, you'll get a bad reference.

Reality

Because of the legal liabilities associated with giving references, most employers won't take a chance and "bad mouth" you.

Discussion

If you fear a former supervisor may say negative things about you, confront him or her. Ask what he or she would say if contacted for a reference. If you're not happy with the answer, don't rely on that person as a reference. Remind them about company policy and laws regarding giving references for former employees.

Examples: Derick Moeller had a rocky relationship with his former boss. Although Moeller had resigned instead of waiting to be fired, he wasn't sure what his former supervisor would say, so he called him.

"My boss and I never got along," said Moeller. "It reached a point where if I hadn't quit, he would have fired me. Then I worried that the jerk would black-ball me from getting another job. I called him, as much as I hated to, and asked him point-blank what he would say if I put his name down as a reference. He told me he would follow company policy and only verify that I had worked there for 3 years and nothing more."

Peter Stanford had a pleasant surprise when he permitted a prospective employer to contact a former supervisor. He learned that the supervisor, with whom Stanford had experienced difficulties, gave him a good reference. When Stanford called to thank him, the man told him that despite their disagreements, he had fully recognized his strengths as an employee and sincerely hoped he'd be happy in his new job. Stanford could have saved himself some worry by checking in with his former supervisor in advance.

Most companies aren't willing to take the risk, or have their employees take the risk, of giving a bad reference that could end up in a legal battle. However, if you want to be absolutely sure what's being said about you, find a reliable ally to "check your references." It's the best way to determine whom you can and cannot trust.

Myth #57

If you're invited for a meal,
you can assume the job is yours.

Reality

It may mean you're getting closer to a job offer, but you could end up losing the job if you don't prepare for this important part of the evaluation.

Discussion

Never assume anything. Consider every minute you spend with the prospective employer part of the interview. There's no magic formula for successful interviewing, but you can lose points (and even the job) if you don't understand certain social protocol in a dining situation.

Some companies may invite the candidate for a meal in an effort to gather additional information. Inappropriate behavior such as talking too much or too loudly or with a mouth full of food could mean the end of further consideration for the job. If the candidate was referred by a recruiter, a lack of common sense or one too many beers could be part of a negative message communicated by the company to the recruiter following the meal.

Another variable is whether the meal is a one-on-one situation (the recruiter, hiring manager, or other company representative and the candidate) or a group affair. For a group meal, the company may invite several candidates at the same time, or may invite a single candidate, but have several company representatives present. The company knows that a candidate who interviewed well in a one-on-one situation may or may not demonstrate strength in a different type of setting.

When a prospective employer invites you for a meal, keep these tips in mind:

- Be ready for small talk.
- Try not to be nervous.
- Don't forget why you're there.
- Watch your body language.
- Maintain good eye contact.
- Avoid alcoholic beverages, or drink in moderation.
- Don't put all your eggs in one basket.

With regard to this last point, sometimes when candidates receive an invitation to dine, they are so positive that a job offer will follow that they become overly confident. Don't lose momentum and stop or slow your job search because of a dinner invitation. You don't have the job until you receive and accept the actual offer.

Every social situation has unwritten rules of behavior, whether it's a cocktail party, a date, or a meal in conjunction with a job interview. When dining with a prospective employer, you'll need to consider such items as what to wear, what to order, appropriate conversation, and whether or not to drink an alcoholic beverage, among other things. Having a meal as part of the interview process is not the same as dinner with family or friends. The employer will observe your behavior in what can be a stressful social situation and use that information as part of the selection process.

Nearly everyone has heard the story of the interviewer who wouldn't hire people who seasoned their food before tasting it because he felt it indicated they prejudged situations. Apparently this is a true "no-no" because business etiquette courses still discuss this today. It's not just the big items that can create a problem, but the small ones as well. Again, consider every minute you spend with the prospective employer part of the interview.

Let's take a look at some of the tricky issues that you'll want to consider.

Attire

If the meal will take place outside regular office hours, the invitation will most likely specify the dress code, such as, "business attire," "business casual," etc. If it does not, it's acceptable to ask the interviewer or the recruiter about appropriate attire.

If the meal is part of the actual interview (that is, you will be in interviews before and after lunch), then dress for the interviews (business attire) and wear that for lunch also. If you're not sure about what to wear to the interview–meal combination, you can't go wrong by dressing professionally.

Introductions

You will very likely meet new people when invited to dine. Keep in mind some basic rules regarding introductions:

- In a business setting, both men and women rise for introductions.
- Both men and women should always shake hands when introduced in a business environment.
- Use a firm handshake that expresses warmth. Don't use the "limp dishrag" grasp; but, don't wring or crush the other person's hand either.
- Make eye contact and smile as you shake hands.
- Include the other person's name in your greeting if possible. If you didn't understand the person's name, say so immediately: "Excuse me, but could you repeat your name?"
- Acknowledge introductions with a simple, "How are you, Mr. Jones," or, "I'm very happy to meet you, Miss Smith," being sure to use their last name only even if their first name was included in the introduction.

What To Order & How Much

The location of the meal is a main consideration when it comes to deciding what to order. In some cases, you may dine in the company dining room. This usually means either a buffet or a limited menu so you don't have to worry as much about what's correct to order. The company may use a pre-determined menu that offers you a choice of several entrees. Dining on-site also eliminates the question of whether to have alcohol with a meal (a bad idea) because most won't offer alcohol in this situation.

In the event the meal takes place elsewhere, wait for your host to take the lead. Some companies advise their people (the hosts) to do this because it gives the candidate an idea of what to order. If your host isn't the first to order, it's perfectly acceptable to ask what he would recommend. Just remember not to order the most expensive item on the menu.

You'll also want to consider the type of food you're ordering and whether it'll be easy or difficult to eat. Choose something that's easy to cut and consume. Barbecued ribs or spaghetti may be your favorite dish, but both are difficult to eat gracefully and you may wind up leaving the meal with a stain on the front of your clothing.

It's also not a good idea to order unfamiliar food. At the extreme, you could have an allergic reaction to a new food; at the least, you may end up trying to choke down food you don't like.

Don't overindulge. Gluttony isn't considered a desirable trait in anyone. It's not necessary to leave your plate free of every trace of food, despite what your mother told you. This isn't the time to belong to the "clean plate club."

On the other hand, don't order lots of food and then waste it. One hapless candidate insisted the waitress bring extra dressing for her salad, and then left most of the salad uneaten and never touched the dressing.

Don't decide to skip the food because you're nervous and don't want to make mistakes. It may create questions about how well you can handle stress. Also, just nibbling at the buffet or meal doesn't count as eating.

Alcohol—To Drink or Not To Drink

Even if you feel comfortable having a glass of wine or a mixed drink with your meal, it's best to decline if it's offered and certainly don't ask if it's not offered. In general, alcohol and interviews don't go together. You may believe alcohol will help you relax and be at your best, but if you relax too much it's very easy to say or do the wrong thing without even realizing what happened. Remember, the meal is still part of the interview process.

Conversation

Conversation in this situation can be tricky. Your goal is to appear calm, relaxed, and friendly. Use this time to express your interest in the company and to learn more about both the company and the position. Keep the tone of your conversation positive. You don't want to come across as someone with a negative view on life in general or as a complainer.

Basically, be cautious about what you discuss. This isn't the time to talk about what went wrong in another job or in another job interview. Avoid discussing personal information. Telling someone about the wild party you attended over the weekend isn't a good idea. Don't open discussions on religion, politics, or other equally controversial topics. If someone else starts the discussion, you can listen politely without commenting, then steer the conversation in another direction as discreetly as possible.

Don't discuss, or brag about, other job opportunities that you have or could have had instead of the job in question. It's unbecoming, inappropriate, and also potentially embarrassing if your "sure fire" job offer doesn't materialize.

Keep in mind that employers are looking for candidates with good communication and interpersonal skills, and a meal is a place to demonstrate your strengths in this area.

Companies aren't just being nice when they invite you for a meal. They're using it as a way to evaluate and screen candidates. They want to see how you react under pressure.

You probably won't lose a job opportunity if you use the wrong fork, but behaving inappropriately is another matter. Speaking to the server rudely or demanding special attention or service will definitely make an impression, but it won't be a good one.

Many schools offer seminars in business etiquette. If you feel uncomfortable about the prospect of dining with a prospective employer or are uncertain about your social skills, it may be worth your time to invest in a class.

You can't change who you are by reading the latest interviewing tips before dining with a prospective employer. However, preparation will give you the confidence to relax and present yourself at your best. That's all you can do, but that's usually enough.

Basic Rules of Dining

Choosing the Right Fork, etc.

- Silverware is usually arranged in the order in which you'll use it. Thus, if you have three forks, you would use the one on the outside first and work your way in toward the plate for different courses.

- Your water glass is the one to your right.
- Your bread and butter plate is the one to your left.
- If there's a spoon/fork at the top of your plate, it's for your dessert.
- Use serving pieces (pickle fork, sugar tongs, nut spoon) instead of your fingers.
- Eat chicken with a knife and fork; fingers are for at home or at picnics. This also applies to French fried potatoes.
- Use a dessert fork to eat pie. Use a dessert fork and a spoon to eat cake a-la-mode.
- Your napkin belongs in your lap. (If you must leave the table you may place the napkin on the seat of your chair.)

When/How Should I... ?

- It's customary to wait for everyone to be served before you begin to eat. If there's a large group (eight or more) you should wait until at least half of the people have been served before you begin. Do the same with dessert.
- If you have to sneeze or cough, turn your head to the side and cover your mouth with your napkin.
- Never use the napkin as a handkerchief for your nose.
- Put only enough food on the fork or spoon for one bite. Don't overload the utensil and then take several bites.
- If you encounter a piece of meat you can't chew, quietly slide it onto your fork and place it on the rim of your plate.
- Remove olive pits, small bones, etc. from your mouth using your thumb and forefinger.
- Foods, even finger foods, belong on your plate, not on the table cloth. This includes sandwiches, olives, raw vegetables (such as carrots and celery), fresh fruit, cookies, etc.
- You may place your elbows on the table between courses as long as no food is at your place. Keeping your hands in your lap between courses will help to reduce the possibility of an accident, such as knocking over your water glass, at the table.
- The hand you aren't using to eat should rest in your lap.
- Break, don't cut, bread or rolls one piece at a time. Butter each piece individually before eating. You may, however, butter hot breads while still hot, then break into smaller pieces.
- Use a knife and fork to eat messy sandwiches.

- If eating corn on the cob, put butter and salt on a few rows at a time. You may hold the ear in both hands.
- Put condiments (ketchup, mustard, jelly, etc.) on your plate. Then transfer them to your food.

Saying the Right Thing

- Remember to say "please" and "thank you."
- Avoid remarks such as, "I'm too full" or "I'm stuffed," and don't discuss diets or food allergies.

A Few Don'ts

- Don't click your coffee cup when stirring your coffee; stir quietly.
- Don't play with the silverware.
- Don't doodle on the tablecloth.
- Don't use your fork as an exclamation point when you talk.
- Don't blow on hot soup or coffee. Let it cool by itself.
- Don't slurp anything.
- Don't speak with food in your mouth.

If you're in a situation where you're totally unsure of which fork or spoon to use, observe your host or hostess and follow his or her example. Hopefully you won't find yourself in the position of the inexperienced young man who didn't know which of the three forks at his place setting to use. He looked around and saw one person pick up the inside fork and another pick up the outside fork. So he picked up the fork in the middle.

After you finish eating the meal, place your knife and fork on your plate. The standard practice today is the "10:20" position. Think of your plate as a clock face. Put the knife and fork in what would be the 10:20 position. The points should be at the "10" and the handles at the "4" (as in 20 minutes past 10 o'clock).

*   *   *

Remember to send a thank you letter after a meal just as you would after an interview.

Myth #58

The company's first offer is their best and last offer.

Reality

Most initial offers are lower than what the company is willing to pay.

Discussion

The toughest part of the job interview is when the talk turns to money. Most job seekers feel uncomfortable talking about salary. Maybe it's because they feel that they need the job more than the job needs them.

You need to get past your feelings of discomfort on this subject. You're not going to be happy several months down the road if you find that others in similar positions, maybe even in your own company, earn more than you.

Review the following as you evaluate a job offer.

Know the least you'd be willing to accept. Consider your living expenses and what others in like jobs earn. Your current salary is also a factor. You may decide not to change jobs or accept an offer unless it means at least a 15 percent increase in base pay. On the other hand, pay may be less important to you than opportunity for growth, travel, benefits, or location. In addition, would you be willing to take a cut in pay for the "right" position?

How you determine your rock bottom price is up to you. The important thing is that you know what you're willing to accept before you start negotiating.

Estimate the organization's top price. The employer always has a salary range in mind. This is vital information. You will want to get every dollar the company is willing to pay. Why wait a year for a $3,000 raise when you could have had it right from the beginning?

Your best source for getting this type of information is from people who already work for the company. You may not want to ask them what they make, but you can ask what they think the position is worth. Other sources include surveys by professional associations such as the American Management Association, recruiters, and people who work in similar positions in other companies.

Time it right. Don't give in to the urge to talk about salary until you get the message from the prospective employer that he's definitely interested in hiring you. Once the employer decides you're right for the job you have some leverage in negotiations. (See Myth #50 for more details.)

Let the interviewer make the first offer. Keep in mind that employers will rarely offer you more than you ask for initially. If you ask for $25,000 and later find that the employer was willing to pay $35,000, it's difficult to retrace your steps and ask for the higher figure.

If the employer knows you're determined to let him or her make the opening bid, in most cases he or she will regard this as a sign of your willingness to be flexible. The employer's time is valuable, so after the question is thrown back a couple of times, he or she will probably provide the first number. If the employer absolutely insists that you state your salary expectations first, you have little choice but to say something. If this happens, state a salary range, not an exact dollar amount.

Use silence to your advantage. After the interviewer makes you an offer, remain silent for a few seconds, giving the impression the offer doesn't particularly excite you. Counter-offer with a figure 15–20 percent over the interviewer's offer and re-emphasize two or three specific qualifications you have that support your counter-offer.

You can't strong-arm an employer into giving you more money, but thorough preparation will help you avoid short-changing yourself.

In the event that you discover the first offer is their only offer and they're not willing to negotiate, then you'll have to decide whether to accept. If you want the job and their offer is acceptable (even though not as much as you wanted), then don't be embarrassed to say "yes."

Myth #59

The best-qualified people get the jobs.

Reality

Candidates who sell themselves effectively in the interviews get the jobs.

Discussion

The personal interview is the most important part of the job search. Every part of the interview process and how you handle it is critical to your success.

Prepare for the interview by researching the organization. Learn as much as you can about the business and the person or persons who will interview you. Locate as much information as possible about the job and what the company is looking for in a candidate. Maybe you have an acquaintance or business associate who knows why the position is currently unfilled. If a recruiter set up the interview, he or she should be able to supply information about the job.

Some companies will actually supply candidates with information about the company and/or the job. This may be true particularly if they're using a recruiter, a job fair, or a school in their employee search. If you get this information, be sure you review it. The employer will be able to determine easily whether or not you read the material. If you didn't care enough to read the material or view the tape, they may decide you're not the person for them.

Another part of your preparation for the interview is to inventory your assets as an employee. What abilities and skills do you plan to emphasize during the interview? Review your resume the day before the interview. Is there anything that you want to be sure to mention in the interview that is not on the resume? Has information changed since you prepared the resume, or have you become aware of additional items you want to emphasize as a result of interviews with other people in the company? Do you need to take work samples to the interview? If so, get them ready.

Try to anticipate some of the questions the interviewer may ask. Prepare for difficult questions, such as why you left a previous employer. Plan to focus on the positive. Decide how you'll utilize your strengths and compensate for any weaknesses. If you've had previous interviews for other jobs, look back at them and analyze what went well and what didn't. If you feel you made mistakes in those interviews, determine the cause.

Do you have your list of references typed and ready to present if the interviewer requests them? Have you contacted all the people you've listed as references?

Think about what questions you'll want to ask during the interview. If necessary write down a few key words to help you focus on your questions. Also be sure to have a pen and notebook to take with you. You'll want to take notes during the interview and asking the interviewer to "loan" you a pen and piece of paper is poor interview etiquette.

Plan your wardrobe for the interview. Is your clothing clean and ready for you to wear? Do you need to polish your shoes? Some of these may seem like simple things, and yet amazingly candidates often don't plan ahead. The morning of the interview they're rushing out for hosiery or shoe polish, or picking up a suit from the cleaners. You don't need unnecessary last-minute pressure.

Do you know how to get to the interview location? This is especially important if you're interviewing out of town and will be driving in unfamiliar territory. How long will it take? You don't want to arrive at the interview at the last minute. If you're driving, does your car have enough gas? This may sound like a basic question, but there are people who have run out of gas on their way to an interview.

Tape a practice interview (with a friend posing as the interviewer) and then use the tape to help you spot areas where you need to improve, or recognize areas where you did well. You may feel somewhat awkward "practicing" for an interview, but you will likely be pleasantly surprised when you realize the benefits during the actual interview.

You may have excellent qualifications, a sterling character, and a wonderful work record, but if the interviewer doesn't discover this while meeting with you, you could lose out to people less qualified who knew how to sell themselves in the interview.

Myth #60

When interviewers say you're overqualified, they really mean you're too old.

Reality

Being told you're overqualified is less a function of age than it is of skills and work experience.

Discussion

If you're hearing the "overqualified" response from interviewers, there are two likely scenarios: (1) you may be overqualified; or (2) you may have a problem with how you present yourself and what you have to offer a prospective employer.

Don't allow yourself to accept the excuse, "It's my age," as the easy explanation for lack of job offers. Candidates of any age must know what skills and attitude managers seek and how to package themselves for the marketplace. In the case of the older candidate, this can be especially important. The business world has little place for candidates with outdated operating methods or a hierarchical mentality.

Keep in mind that on occasion you might apply for a job for which you are truly overqualified. If you've researched the company and position, however, these instances should be rare.

Employers who hire an overqualified person for a job (e.g., a Ph.D. for an entry-level position) realize it's likely that the person will soon start looking for a more challenging position. This then leaves the employer with a vacancy to fill once again, and that's expensive. So most employers are understandably hesitant to hire overqualified candidates unless there are extenuating circumstances.

Older candidates actually have several things in their favor. Many hiring managers look for candidates who appear to be overachievers. They want candidates with a strong work ethic. In this situation, the older job candidates often have an advantage. They frequently have fewer family demands, which leaves them more time to concentrate on their work.

The older candidate has also had the opportunity to establish a track record through previous employment. If you spent most of your career with one company, however, focus on what you've accomplished in the last 7 or 8 years there. Demonstrate to the interviewer or hiring manager that you have the knowledge and skills needed to function in the current business climate. Know what specific skills and experience you have to offer in relationship to the job for which you're interviewing and sell that to the interviewer. Relate specific examples from your recent past.

If you apply for a position in a small company, remember that in such companies each employee often wears several "hats" and everyone pitches in, regardless of rank or title. The interviewer will try to determine whether you're willing to be a team player or more interested in giving orders. You may also have to take a cut in pay even for a similar level of responsibility. If you convey to the interviewer that either of these is unacceptable, you may hear the word "overqualified."

It's not unusual for job applicants to face an interviewer who's younger than them. The important thing is to realize this may happen and mentally prepare yourself. Candidates in this situation sometimes have a tendency to feel the need to justify their age. Don't start the interview by explaining why your age shouldn't be a factor. If you make an issue of your age, the interviewer may begin to wonder why. Older candidates also need to avoid letting their own perception that there's an age problem cause them to actually reinforce any negative stereotypes the interviewer may already have.

There's an old saying, "Age is simply a case of mind over matter. If you don't mind, it doesn't matter." When you interview for a job, put your age out of your mind. Present your qualifications and the reason why you would be the perfect match for the job. You have a better chance of not being discriminated against because of age by knowing and following the rules of today's job market.

The Top Ten Reasons Candidates Are Rejected

1. **Not qualified**—You have nothing to lose by applying for jobs that look like a match, but if you overstate your qualifications it will be apparent in the interview.
2. **Lack of enthusiasm**—You don't have to be Zig Ziglar or Richard Simmons, but you must express enthusiasm for the job. Otherwise, the interviewer will question your attitude, and may exclude you from further consideration.
3. **Poor interpersonal skills**—You may look great on paper, but if you don't have the ability to work well on a team and get along with others, you'll be viewed as a bad choice. For example, answers that indicate you've had disagreements with teammates could be reason for the interviewer to eliminate you from consideration. Although there are times when we don't agree with others, the interview is neither the time nor the place to bring up this information.
4. **A "what's in it for me" mindset**—Every employer wants to know what you can do for them. Giving the impression that your only interest is in salary and benefits, instead of what you can contribute to the job, turns most employers off.
5. **Unclear job goals**—Know what you want. If you're going through some soul searching, don't reveal it during the interview. Implying that you're uncertain about your goals leaves the interviewer with the impression that you'd be a risk, someone that might quit if something better comes along. Businesses don't need employees who hire on and then soon leave because it's not what they really wanted in a job.
6. **"Bad mouthing" previous employers**—Your attitude toward a former manager could be your downfall. Don't try to evoke sympathy from the interviewer, or get even with a former supervisor, by describing him or her as "unfair," "incompetent," or "unwilling to give me a break." Sour grapes reflects poorly on you, not your employer.
7. **Poor personal appearance**—You may think you look great in leather pants, a see-through blouse, outrageous jewelry, or a spiked haircut.

However, if the interviewer doesn't agree with you, you've lost an opportunity. Poor manners, bad breath, or an appearance that's too casual are also reasons an interviewer may reject you.

8. **Not selling yourself**—Promote yourself. Know your strengths and be able to explain during the interview why the position interests you and why you're capable of handling the job. You are your own best advertisement. If you can't sell yourself, no one can.

9. **Unprepared for the interview**—It's always obvious when a candidate isn't prepared for the interview. What you haven't done speaks volumes about you. Understand what the company does and know what you have to offer the company. It always impresses interviewers when you know something about their business. The more you know about them, the better.

10. **Revealing weaknesses**—One of the primary jobs of the hiring manager is to find your weaknesses. Within 30 minutes, a thorough screening by a skilled interviewer will reveal a lot about you. Don't volunteer weaknesses, such as being a procrastinator, not paying attention to detail, or having been criticized for the way you handle breakdowns in communication. Present only your best side. Everyone has weaknesses, but offering to share them with the interviewer is a mistake.

Myth #61

There's no such thing as job security.

Reality

The best way to keep your job is to become indispensable. Take steps now to make yourself a valued employee.

Discussion

There's no guarantee that you'll never get a pink slip. Even the best employees are sometimes swept away in reorganizations or petty company politics. However, your chances for keeping your job as others around you are losing theirs, are much better if your employer believes that you're an indispensable part of the operation. The time to do things that foster that belief is now.

Become an expert in your job—Mark Canosa, a training and safety coordinator, believes there are several ways to become an expert and a more valued employee. "First, understand the business of which you are a part. The more you know, the more credible you are in the eyes of your employer. Second, find out what the major goals of the organization are. Then, develop your specific goals to support those goals. Third, get creative and look for ways that you can learn from others."

Find out what goes on in other departments—Don't stop with becoming an expert in your own job. Employees who understand the big picture are more likely to be in a position to help others do their jobs well and be remembered for their helpfulness.

Strengthen your relationship with your supervisor—As with any relationship, the chemistry between you and your supervisor is unique. He or she may be affable and easygoing, or aloof and formal. You can't change his or her style, but, within reason, you should try to make the working relationship comfortable and productive. Although that might seem obvious, the number of people who cultivate an adversarial relationship with their supervisor, arguing at every turn and making their disrespect obvious, might surprise you. Even if you have a boss you don't like, you need to make the best of the situation or start looking for another job.

Be positive—How others perceive you is important to your success. If you're a complainer or have a negative attitude, you close the door on opportunities. Employers want to hire and keep people who not only are technically competent, but also have a positive outlook.

Become active in your profession—If you're not already involved in professional or trade associations, start attending meetings. The more people you know, the stronger your safety net. Some people feel they don't have time to participate in such outside activities. But you need to make the time, even if it takes time away from working hours that are not required. If you lose your job, you'll need contacts outside your organization.

Be flexible—It's natural for people to resist change sometimes, especially if the change involves technology that seems difficult to learn. However, business moves quickly; if you're going to be a player you've got to move with it. Don't be labeled as one of those people time has passed by.

Become a team player—Very few of us have positions that operate completely independently of others. If you're late, it usually delays someone else. If you do a sloppy job, someone has to correct your mistakes. When things go wrong, it's not easy to pin the blame on one person. Your whole department or your supervisor may get the blame if a project fails. If you don't pull your own weight, your peers will regard you as a liability, someone that could sabotage their careers. If this is the case, be assured they'll start looking for ways to undermine you and get you out the door.

Blow your own horn—Self-marketing is a continuous process and a vital part of maintaining a competitive advantage. It doesn't mean being boastful, arrogant, pushy, or egotistical. Self-promotion can be done with class and honesty and should be based on genuine respect and concern for the needs of others.

Strengthen your communication skills—Businesses are crying out for people with good communication skills. If you have these abilities, leverage them by volunteering for writing or speaking assignments. If you're a little weak in this area, look for ways to improve.

Learn to set goals—If you don't know where you're going, how will you know if you're making progress? If you have resigned yourself to being someone who just shows up for work and puts in your time, don't worry about goals. If you want something more, set goals and make plans.

Go the extra mile—It can make a difference in the way people perceive you. It might require taking on extra work, volunteering to help on a project, putting in overtime, or being willing to cross-train in another department. There are plenty of opportunities to reach out and help others. Employees who have the attitude, "It's not my job," are the losers in more ways than one.

The things you do today to strengthen your career safety net could potentially save your job in the future.

APPENDICES

A Sample Accomplishment Statements

B Internet Glossary

C Job Lead Organizations

D Pre-Employment Inquiries

E Sample Interview Questions and Answers

Sample Accomplishment Statements

As you prepare your resume you will want to write accomplishment statements. This exercise will also help you organize your thoughts.

Accomplishment statements start with an action verb and tell employers what contributions you've made in the past. They support the fact that you have the abilities and skills to complete certain tasks as well as have the potential for solving problems.

Write in terms of contributions, impact, and skills. Many people use resumes written in the form of job descriptions; they describe what they did but not how well they did it.

Here are some examples of accomplishment statements:

For Operations

- Led JIT effort to reduce assembly cycle time by half in the transformer assembly area.
- Developed methods and layout that doubled throughput of units through control wiring.
- Implemented over $1 million in cost reductions in laboratory and polymer areas of chemical plant.
- Designed and implemented waste reclamation project that reclaimed over 1 million pounds of waste polyester per year.

- Designed and implemented absentee control program for 100 hourly employees that reduced overall absenteeism by 55 percent in 1998.
- Consolidated warehouse distribution procedures and achieved an average annual cost savings of $275,000 each year for 10 years.
- Promoted a new concept in quality control procedures that reduced labor costs by $250,000 annually for each of five years.
- Achieved the lowest accident rate of three plants for four consecutive years.

For Human Resources

- Challenged OSHA citation with potential resolution cost of $50,000; secured settlement without cost to company.
- Bargained union to de-certification with rejection of 78 percent.
- Settled "no win" arbitration at no cost or restriction to company.
- Negotiated group health insurance plan that increased protection tenfold while reducing premium costs by 27 percent.
- Achieved savings of $800,000 in benefits administration for 1998 through program redesign and system-wide consolidation.
- Reduced turnover by 46% through management and organizational development strategies between 1994 and 1998.
- Designed Alternative Dispute Resolution (ADR) methodologies that reduced complaints, grievances, and EEO charges by 50% for 1996–1998.

For Sales

- Negotiated and closed 11 percent of all sales in 1998—20.5 million dollars.
- Increased sales from $1 million in 1994 to $5 million by 1998.
- Reduced receivables from 45 days to 30 days.
- Reduced average monthly back-orders from $500,000 to $25,000 while reducing inventory by 30 percent within 1 year.
- Developed export strategy to expand sales with new product lines that increased revenues by $2 million from 1995 to 1998.
- Identified and developed new business opportunities to achieve $750,000 in sales in 1998.

- Re-negotiated a corporate price increase that still resulted in a client retention rate in excess of 89 percent.
- Improved productivity in customer call center by 25 percent by introducing new policies and procedures.

The following action verbs are a sample of what you can use for the first word of your accomplishment statements:

Accelerated	Accomplished	Achieved	Adapted
Administered	Analyzed	Approved	Budgeted
Built	Conceived	Conducted	Conferred
Consolidated	Contacted	Controlled	Converted
Coordinated	Created	Cut	Delegated
Delivered	Demonstrated	Designed	Developed
Devised	Directed	Doubled	Earned
Edited	Effected	Eliminated	Established
Evaluated	Exhibited	Expanded	Expedited
Forecasted	Formulated	Founded	Generated
Guided	Handled	Headed	Implemented
Improved	Improvised	Installed	Instituted
Introduced	Increased	Influenced	Invented
Launched	Led	Maintained	Managed
Negotiated	Operated	Organized	Originated
Oversaw	Participated	Performed	Planned
Presented	Produced	Programmed	Proposed
Provided	Recommended	Reduced	Reinforced
Re-negotiated	Reorganized	Researched	Reviewed
Revised	Scheduled	Settled	Set up
Simplified	Sold	Solved	Sparked
Spearheaded	Staffed	Started	Streamlined
Strengthened	Stretched	Structured	Succeeded
Supervised	Supported	Systematized	Taught
Terminated	Traced	Tracked	Traded
Trained	Transferred	Transformed	Translated
Trimmed	Tripled	Uncovered	Unified
Utilized	Won	Worked	Wrote

B | Internet Glossary

Access provider: A group or organization that will connect you to the Internet, such as America Online, CompuServe, or Prodigy.

Bookmark: An electronic reminder of an Internet address. If you find a particularly helpful job-search site, bookmark it for later or repeated use.

Browser: Software that allows you to access sites on the Internet.

Cyberspace: Jargon for the Internet universe.

Download: To take information from a site on the Internet.

E-mail: The abbreviation for "electronic mail" sent from one computer to another via the Internet or within an organization.

Home page: An organization's main page on its Web site. The home page provides links from it to other parts of the site.

Information Superhighway: Jargon for the Internet.

Internet: An electronic network of millions of computers.

Intranet: An organization's internal electronic network.

Listserv: A group of people who discuss issues via e-mail. When one person sends a message to the "list," the listserv software sends the message to all subscribers.

Network: A series of connected computers.

On-line: Signed onto a computer and accessing the Internet.

Password: A word, number, or combination of the two that allows you access to a computer, a database, or a site on the World Wide Web.

Upload: To send information to another computer.

Web site: An organization's electronic collection on the Internet.

World Wide Web or WWW: A network of Web sites on the Internet.

Job Lead Organizations

ARIZONA
American Career Group
2400 E. Arizona Biltmore Circle, Bldg. 2, Suite 2250, Phoenix, AZ 85015
602-381-1667
Job search program for professionals, executives, and recent college graduates.
Fee.

ARKANSAS
Arkansas Employment Security Department, Dislocated Worker Resource Center
616 Garrison, Room 101, P.O. Box 1987, Fort Smith, AK 72909
501-783-0231
Job search assistance through the Automated Labor Exchange (ALEX).
Resume and cover letter preparation; use of fax, copier, and computers; for
laid-off workers. No charge.

CALIFORNIA
John F. Kennedy University Career Development Center
1250 Arroyo Way, Walnut Creek, CA 94596
510-295-0610
Workshops, career counseling, self-assessment, testing; resource library offers
job listings updated weekly, information on companies for interview preparation, and books on career planning and job search. Daily fee: $3; yearly
membership includes discounts on workshops, counseling, and free access
to the resource center.

The Job Forum
Walnut Creek Chamber of Commerce
1501 North Broadway, Suite 410, Walnut Creek, CA 94596
415-934-2007
Group meets first and third Tuesday of every month, 7:00–9:00 p.m.

Professional Experience Network
California Employment Development Department
480 Mountain View Avenue, San Bernardino, CA 92408
714-383-4106
Support group and job club for professionals seeking employment. Workshops on resume writing, interviewing strategies, and career marketing skills.

Forty Plus of Southern California
3450 Wilshire Boulevard, Suite 510, Los Angeles, CA 90010
213-388-2301
Offers career marketing techniques in the Los Angeles, Orange County, and San Diego areas on Wednesdays at 10:00 a.m. for executives and professionals over 40.

Central Valley Professionals
Chapter of Experience Unlimited
California Employment Development Department
1455 East Shaw, Fresno, CA 93710-8001
209-244-7626
Self-help job search and networking club for professionals; training and assistance in resume preparation, self-marketing, and job interview techniques.

Turning Point Career Center
University YMCA, 2600 Bancroft Way, Berkeley, CA 94704
510-848-6370
Drop-in support group for job seekers and career changers, Thursdays from 4:00 to 5:00 p.m.; participants share feedback and support for maintaining motivation, refining job-search skills, or resolving problems encountered in the job search. Fee.

Women's Opportunities Center
University of California, Irvine, P.O. Box 6050, Irvine, CA 92616
714-824-7128

Membership career counseling center for women and men seeking a new job or career change; services include job-search groups, workshops, and seminars, resource library, Internet access, job listings, and peer support groups; job search support group meetings held twice every Monday. First session is free.

Experience Unlimited of San Francisco
745 Franklin Street, San Francisco, CA 94102
415-771-1776
Self-help job club for professionals; call weekdays, 9:00 a.m. to 4:30 p.m.

PRONET, Fremont Chapter of Experience Unlimited, Employment Development Department
39155 Liberty Street, Suite 107, Fremont, CA 94538
510-794-3716
Volunteer organization for professionals; Monday–Friday, 8:30 a.m. to 4:30 p.m.; introduction session, Fridays at 9:00 a.m.; job search, interview, and resume writing workshops weekly; resources include employer information, computers, telephones, fax, peer networking and referral opportunities. No charge.

Networking Experience Unlimited, State of California Employment Development Department
933 S. Glendora Avenue, West Covina, CA 91790
818-814-8291
Job club offering job matching service for unemployed professionals and training in using the Internet to find work, researching companies, job search techniques, resume writing, interviewing, and time and budget management for the employed. No charge.

COLORADO
Forty Plus of Colorado Inc.
5800 W. Alameda Avenue, Lakewood, CO 80226
303-937-4956
Non-profit organization for professionals over 40; 4-day training class on networking, resume writing, and interviewing; job search support and services; meets Mondays at 9:15 a.m.

Forty Plus of Colorado Springs Inc.
255 Airport Road, Colorado Springs, CO 80910-3176
719-473-6220
Weekly meetings, Tuesdays at 9:00 a.m.; resume preparation, interviewing techniques, and networking; word processing, fax, and photocopying equipment available. Monthly dues: $25.

Career Counseling Services Inc.
7114 West Jefferson Avenue, Suite 309, Lakewood, CO 80235
303-703-0210
Workshop: "Fight Phone Fear and Win", second Tuesday monthly, essential phone skills for a successful job search; fee: $20; pre-registration recommended; call or fax for free information packet for those relocating to Denver.

Epilepsy Foundation of Colorado
234 Columbine Street, Suite 333, Denver, CO 80206
303-377-9774
Non-profit organization offering intensive job training, employment leads, networking opportunities, and home-based business start-up advice for persons with epilepsy. No charge.

CONNECTICUT
Career Transition Support Group
Christ Episcopal Church
254 E. Putnam Avenue, Greenwich, CT 06830
203-869-6600
Participants share job search ideas and strategies, networking contacts, and experience; includes occasional guest speakers; meets Mondays, 7:00–9:30 p.m.

DELAWARE
Westminster Employment Guidance Group
Westminster Presbyterian Church
1304 West 13th Street, Wilmington, DE 19806
302-654-5214
Offers instruction, guidance, guest speakers, support, job leads, and motivation groups for people seeking or changing jobs or careers; meets Mondays, 7:00–9:00 p.m.

FLORIDA

Center for Career Decisions
Town Executive Center, 6100 Glades Road, Suite 210, Boca, Raton, FL 33434
561-470-9333
Action job strategies for displaced or burned-out professionals; nationally certified career counselors will meet by appointment to help you look at your options in changing careers; they offer testing and career counseling as well as help with resumes and networking. Fee.

GEORGIA

Career Development Center of Northeast Georgia
P.O. Box 6833, Athens, GA 30604
706-354-4690
For people in need of job search assistance and strategy planning; lunch and learn sessions are on Wednesdays, 12:00–1:00 p.m.; topics covered include networking, information interviewing, resume development, and interviewing techniques. Fee: $10 per session.

Career Quest
Adult Education Center, Catholic Church of St. Ann
4905 Roswell Road N.E., Marietta, GA 30062
770-552-6402 or 770-998-1373
Job search workshops include creative tools and practical courses for employees at risk and anyone requiring job search assistance, 7:45–10:00 p.m. Tuesdays.

Career Transition Ministry
St. Anne's Espiscopal Church
3098 Northside Parkway N.W., Atlanta, GA 30327
404-237-5589
Career focusing, resumes, networking strategies, interviewing workshops, and personalized assistance, 7:30–9:30 p.m. Thursdays.

Resumes, Resources, Readiness
Callaway Auditorium
Shepherd Center, 2020 Peachtree Road N.W., Atlanta, GA 30309
404-350-7585
Employment workshop for people with disabilities provides guidance in preparing a resume, improving interviewing skills, working through the application process, and better understanding of what companies are looking for in candidates for employment.

HAWAII
Career Search Network Group
711 Kapiolani Blvd., Suite 120, Honolulu, HI 96813
808-591-4940
Job search support and networking group for people seeking careers in clerical, office, or professional positions; third Wednesday monthly; speakers, networking opportunities, workshops, and seminars; 6 months' previous work experience required; call for reservations.

ILLINOIS
Career Services
Elgin Community College
1700 Spartan Drive, Elgin, IL 60123-7193
847-888-7399
Work one-on-one with career specialists to explore how your interests fit with various career areas, or to improve your resume and write letters for the job search; computer-assisted job search help is also available.

Career Transition Center
William Rainey Harper College
1375 South Wolf Road, Prospect Heights, IL 60070
847-925-6000
Offers full-service career resource center as well as workshops, career counseling, and testing to job or career changers, those looking to enhance present careers, and individuals who have lost their jobs.

LOUISIANA
Career Resource Center
2515 Canal Street, Suite 201, New Orleans, LA 70119
504-822-0800
Offers seminars for people who are unemployed or interested in changing jobs.

Active Career Search
2955 Ridgelake Drive, Suite 112, Metairie, LA 70002
504-838-9959
Job search workshops for professionals in career transition; includes writing resumes and cover letters, interviewing and negotiating skills. Fee: $20 per session; call for reservations.

MARYLAND
Professional Outplacement Assistance Center
Airport Square Building 9, 901 Elkridge Landing Road,
    Linthicum, MD 21090-2920
410-859-3499
Provides services for unemployed professionals, technical, and managerial employees. Offers information on job search networking, resumes, and cover letters; women's issues, personal marketing, and communications seminars; reference resources; computer lab; professional career counseling; telemarketing work stations, resume classified services, and job clubs. Individuals must be referred by the Maryland State Job Service or Job Training Partnership Act Service Delivery Area; all consultations are by appointment only.

MASSACHUSETTS
Radcliffe Career Programs
Cronkite Graduate Center, 6 Ash Street, Cambridge, MA 02138
617-495-8631
Offers a variety of workshops, seminars, and conferences; open to the public. Call to be put on mailing list, or check Web page at <http://www.radcliffe.edu/career/index.html>.

Jewish Vocational Services
105 Chauncy Street, Boston, MA 02111
617-451-8147
Free comprehensive, 4-month training programs offered in automated accounting and medical business skills in Newtonville location; to qualify participants must become eligible and live in the Metro South/West region, and for business/medical skills be at least 55 years of age. Call 617-630-8090 to register.

Experience Unlimited
99 First Street, Cambridge, MA 02141
617-354-4102
A non-profit organization that helps professionals 45 years or older who are seeking part-time or contract work or who are looking for a full-time position in their field.

Swampscott Job Search Support Group
St. John the Evangelist Church
Colman Hall, Humphrey Street, Swampscott, MA 01907

508-745-2592
Free non-sectarian support group offering job search skills, support, networking, and guest speakers; Wednesdays, 7:30–9:00 p.m.

MINNESOTA
Forty Plus of Minnesota Inc.
14870 Granada Avenue, Suite 315, St. Paul, MN 55124
612-681-5919
Offers open meetings for experienced executives, managers, and professionals undergoing career change, Tuesdays at 7:00 p.m. at St. Paul's Church-on-the-Hill, 1524 Summit Avenue, St. Paul.

MISSOURI
Businesspersons Between Jobs
601 E. Claymont Drive, St. Louis, MO 63011
314-394-1440
A self-help group for white-collar professionals meets Mondays, 9:00 a.m. to 12:00 p.m.; offers speakers, interviewing practice sessions, and resume reviews. Lifetime membership fee: $25.

St. Andrew's Episcopal Church
6401 Womall Terrace, Kansas City, MO 64113
816-523-1602
Meets Mondays, 10:00–11:30 a.m.; offers expert speakers, group support, and search materials.

NEBRASKA
Experience Unlimited
5404 Cedar Street, Omaha, NE 68016
402-595-3008
Organization for unemployed or underemployed professional, managerial, and technical job seekers; holds meetings the first Thursday of each month at 9:00 a.m. at the West Hills Presbyterian Church, 82nd and Hascal Streets. Training for resume writing, office techniques, and employer visitations are provided at no charge to members or employees.

Experience Unlimited
P.O. Box 94949, c/o Job Service, 1010 "N" Street, Lincoln, NE 68509
402-471-2275

Meetings providing free support, networking, and education for unemployed professionals at the "N" Street location Thursdays at noon.

NEVADA
Pro-Net, Northern Nevada Professional Network
560 Mill Street #240, Reno, NV 89502
702-688-1680
Self-help networking group of management and professional people seeking to re-enter the job market; weekly meetings, workshops, networking, and educational opportunities.

NEW HAMPSHIRE
Seacoast Job Support Group
c/o Bethel Assembly of God, Market Street at Rt. 95, Portsmouth, NH 03801
603-436-8815
Provides assistance to unemployed or underemployed individuals; meets every Wednesday at 7:00 p.m.; offers instruction in job search basics, with tutoring in resume writing, networking methods, cover letters, and interviewing skills. No charge.

NEW JERSEY
Professional Service Group (PSG)
28 Yard Avenue, Suite 212, CN 058, Trenton, NJ 08625-0058
609-882-5561
A non-profit volunteer self-help organization with a membership base made up of displaced professionals and corporate executives; provides free job search workshops, interactive practice sessions, and an office facility to conduct a job search.

The Professional Services Group
5 Sussex Avenue, Morristown, NJ 07960
201-631-6327
Voluntary, non-profit, self-managing association of unemployed professionals from various disciplines; new members must attend five 3-hour sessions for five consecutive days; sessions cover dealing with unemployment, networking/telephone techniques, resumes/cover letters, and more.

Basil Rouskas Associates
100 Davidson Avenue, Somerset, NJ 08873
908-560-8811
A free career support group is offered on Wednesdays, 6:00–8:00 p.m.; call for schedule.

Job Seekers
St. John's Episcopal Church, 55 Montclair Avenue, Montclair, NJ 07042
201-746-2474
Free meetings on Wednesdays, 7:30–9:30 p.m. for participants to explore the various aspects of the job search, under leadership of volunteer coordinators.

NEW YORK
Rockland County Guidance Center
83 Main Street, Nyack, NY 10960
914-358-9390
Walk-in vocational testing every Monday at 12:00 p.m. and the first Monday of each month at 7:00 p.m.; large career library available at no charge; call for schedule of Wednesday morning workshop series.

Sales & Marketing Career Network
P.O. Box 1269 Port Chester, NY 10573
212-741-6300
Specialists in the sales/marketing field present seminars and networking events for experienced and entry-level job seekers and individuals in career transition interested in the sales profession; meetings conducted in NYC Tuesday evenings at 7:00 p.m.; career counseling also available; call for information and reservations.

NORTH CAROLINA
Carolina Job Network
c/o Britt Grant Associates
5505 Creedmore Road, Suite 109, Raleigh, NC 27612
919-870-0802
A self-help group of unemployed and underemployed professionals; meet on Mondays, 12:00–2:00 p.m.; designed to enhance networking and on-the-job search skills.

Triad Job Search Network
1526 Skeet Club Road, High Point, NC 27265
910-333-1677
A self-help group of unemployed and underemployed professionals; meet every Tuesday, 12:00–2:00 p.m. to network and improve other job search skills.

OHIO
Career Initiatives Center
155 East 27th Street, Cleveland, OH 44114
216-574-8998
Nonprofit organization of members seeking professional, managerial, and technical employment who join together for the purpose of mutual support, education, and assistance during career transition; offers near-downtown office space, computers, copier, fax, phone answering service, database, group support, workshops, and reference library.

Infoplace Services
Cuyahoga County Public Library
5225 Library Lane, Maple Heights, OH 44137
216-475-2225
Provides professional career guidance, job search assistance, and educational information and referral; call for information or appointment. No charge.

Hyde Park Job Search Focus Group
1345 Grace Avenue, Cincinnati, OH 45208
513-871-0320
Member-operated service offering resources and support facilities for professional, managerial, and technical people in the process of job searching or career changing; meets Mondays, 9:00–11:00 a.m. and the third Tuesday of every month at 6:30 p.m.; call for information. Donation supported.

Quality Services International, Inc.
5550 W. Central Avenue, Suite G, Toledo, OH 43615
419-535-9555
Offers an introduction to consulting seminar presented by Consultants Networking Association of America; call for dates and times. No charge.

OKLAHOMA

Job Support Center
4646 South Harvard Avenue, Tulsa, OK 74135
918-742-8700
Offers support and outplacement services for people in career transition; sessions are weekdays, 8:30 a.m. to 5:00 p.m.; call for weekly events schedule. Fee: $25.

OREGON

Job Finders Support Group
c/o 13580 S.W. Ash Avenue, Tigard, OR 97223-4943
503-326-3057
Meets Fridays, 12:00–2:00 p.m., at Capital Hill Library, 10723 S.W. Capitol Highway, Portland; no reservation required. No charge.

Oregon Employment Department
12901 S.W. Jenkins Road, Suite C, Beaverton, OR 97995
503-644-1229
Employment services including job listings, job matching, and job referrals; resource library, videos, computers, and printers; weekly workshops on resumes, interviewing, and networking. No charge.

Lansky Career Consultants
9335 S.W. Capitol Highway, Portland, OR 92719
503-293-0245
Worshops on career direction, resumes, networking, and interviewing; various weekdays, 7:00–9:00 p.m. Fee: $25.

SE Works, Neighborhood Jobs Center
6927 S.W. Foster Road, Portland, OR 97206
503-774-4650
Job search assistance for residents of S.E. Portland; workshops on resumes, interviewing, cover letters, and applications; consultation with a personal advocate; employer information, job listings, screening, and job referrals; resource library; computer and printers; call for schedule. No charge.

PENNSYLVANIA

Enterprising Interns Inc.
222 Lancaster Avenue, Devon, PA 19333

215-254-0249
Offers a free "So you need a job—How can you be the winner?" workshop the first and third Tuesday of each month; call for reservations and times.

Club Job L*I*N*K
CareerPro, Inc.
607 North Easton Road, D-1, Willow Grove, PA 19090
215-830-0530
Job search seminars for both employed and unemployed. Fees and $10 per session for first six seminars; $5 for the next six; then no charge for remaining seminars.

Job Searchers
397 Tyler Run Road, York, PA 17403
717-854-4278
A non-profit volunteer resource group for unemployed white-collar workers in south central Pennsylvania and northern Maryland; weekly meetings held Thursdays at 8:00 a.m. at Aldersgate United Methodist Church in York, PA; free services include weekly guest speakers and workshops to enhance job search skills and to provide emotional support, networking board for unadvertised jobs, resource center, counseling, and individual help.

SOUTH CAROLINA
Job Seekers Club
First Nazarene Church
1201 Haywood Road, Greenville, SC 29615
803-370-9453
Career Counselor Services, Inc. conducts a Job Seekers Club each Monday, 7:00–8:30 p.m.; open to anyone seeking a job; includes networking, job hunting skills, and psychological and spiritual support. No charge.

TENNESSEE
Career Support Ministry
Christ United Methodist Church
4488 Poplar Avenue, Memphis, TN 38117
901-761-0576
A career support breakfast is held on Tuesdays at 6:30 a.m. for people in job transition; free career transition seminars are offered monthly; call for schedule and reservations.

TEXAS

Forty Plus of Houston
2909 Hillcroft, Suite 400, Houston, TX 77057
713-952-7587
Non-profit job search cooperative open to executives, managers, and professionals; instruction and counseling in job search strategies, resume writing, and interviewing; job bank and networking group computers and on-line company research.

Career and Recovery Resources Inc.
2525 San Jacinto, Houston, TX 77002
713-754-7000
Non-profit, comprehensive job search and career change assistance; workshops on job search skills, interviewing, and resumes; job listings, resource center, fax, telephones, and job referral; no qualifications or restrictions for general program. No charge.

Specialized assistance for people with disabilities, people 55 years old and over, and people who are deaf or hard of hearing. No charge.

Jewish Family Service
13140 Coit Road, Suite 400, Dallas, TX 75240
972-437-9950
Employment research group meets the second Tuesday monthly, 7:30–9:00 p.m.; speakers on career development and job search issues; networking opportunities. No charge.

Job search research center; Metroplex job leads, networking, and career information; library computers, phone at no cost, and Internet job banks; fax and copier for nominal fee.

Career guidance, testing, and assessment; resume/cover letter and re-employment assistance available at sliding scale fee.

Interfaith Training and Employment Project, Dislocated Worker Program
2411 Fountainview, Suite 201, Houston, TX 77057-4803
713-953-9211
Job search assistance, fax, WATS line, career assessment/vocational counseling, library, resume and cover letter typing, use of copiers and computers; some funded retraining services. No charge.

Career Center
Corpus Christi Public Libraries
805 Comanche, Corpus Christi, TX 78401
512-880-7000
Offers a free job support group, Mondays, 9:00–10:30 a.m., as well as job listings, business resources, career examination, educational information, professional career guidance, and job search assistance and referral; call for additional information.

Resource Dallas Job Leads Network
Wilshire Baptist Church, 4316 Abrams Road, Rm. 154, Dallas, TX 75214
214-407-4473
Allows unemployed attorneys and financial professionals to exchange job leads, share contract work information, network, and provide job search resources; free CPE credit available for CPAs; meets Wednesdays 9:00–11:00 a.m. Membership is free and dress is professional.

Texas Workforce Commission
1602 16th Street, Lubbock, TX 79410
806-763-6416
Job Search Seminar presented one day each week from 9:00 a.m. to 5:00 p.m.; topics include: building success into the job search, developing an effective promotional package, job campaign strategies, and interview preparation; call for seminar dates, information, and registration. No charge.

Job Search Center
Texas Employment Commission, 2901 Wilcrest #100, Houston, TX 77042
713-784-6656
Workshop and work search sessions stressing interview, networking, resume writing, and telemarketing techniques; research, telephone, and copier facilities available; call for details.

The San Antonio Job Club, Inc.
5825 Callaghan Road, Suite 200, San Antonio, TX 78265
512-680-4010
Programs include job search skills training, weekly roundtables and seminars, computer software training, and counseling; job search workshops are run monthly.

UTAH
Forty Plus of Utah Inc.
5735 South Redwood Road, Room 2907, Salt Lake City, UT 84145
801-269-4797
Non-profit job-seeking membership organization for over-40 executives, professionals, and managers; membership benefits include training, job search marketing, and computer, Internet, fax, phone, and office use; call for fees and schedule.

VIRGINIA
Jobs! Ministry
The Falls Church (Episcopal), 115 East Fairfax Street, Falls Church, VA 22046
703-532-7600
Offers a free job search and support program for those seeking jobs or new career directions; meets Tuesdays at 7:30 p.m.

WASHINGTON
Career Improvement Group
4010 Stone Way Avenue, Suite 200, Seattle, WA 98103
206-545-1155
     or
10900 N.E. 8th, Suite 900, Bellevue, WA 98004
206-451-7996
Job-finding workshops, Tuesdays, 6:00–9:30 p.m. No charge.

Forty Plus of Puget Sound
914 140th Avenue N.E., Suite 100, Bellevue, WA 98005
425-450-0040
Non-profit job search assistance for executives, managers, and professionals; instruction in job search strategies, resume writing, interviewing, and free 1-hour computer orientation, Tuesdays at 2:00 p.m. and 7:00 p.m. and Thursdays at 2:00 p.m.

WASHINGTON, D.C.
Forty Plus of Greater Washington D.C.
1719 P Street N.W., Washington, DC 20036
202-387-1582

Helps unemployed executives with job search techniques; membership meetings are held every Monday at 10:00 a.m.

WISCONSIN

Job Forum
Wauwatosa Savings & Loan, 27th & College, Oak Creek, WI 53154
414-281-8242
Group meets Wednesdays, 7:00–9:30 p.m., discussing a different job search topic every meeting; drop-ins are encouraged. No charge.

WYOMING

Wyoming Department of Employment
851 Werner Court, Casper, WY 82601
307-234-4591
Job search seminars cover resumes, interviews, community resources, and government programs; call for schedule. No charge.

D Pre-Employment Inquiries

Most managers know that there are certain questions that should not be asked during the interview, because they violate Equal Employment Opportunity laws and regulations. However, it's not always obvious which questions are acceptable and which are discriminatory. The following questions provide an overview but are not intended to be all-inclusive. In addition, there are individual state laws that govern what employers may and may not ask during an interview, which of course would vary according to where the interview takes place.

Job seekers can do one of three things when asked to respond to an inappropriate or illegal question:

1. Forego your civil rights and answer the question.
2. Answer without answering. For example, if asked: *"What will your spouse think about your traveling?"* You can respond with: *"Travel has never been a problem for me."* Or *"Who will take care of your children while you are at work?"* You could say: *"I never let personal commitments interfere with my professional life."*
3. Refuse to answer. You could say something like: *"I'm sorry, but I consider that question an invasion of my privacy and I will not answer it."*

The following list of pre-employment inquiries are presented by subject and include what's acceptable and what is considered inappropriate. Laws change, so these may not be all-inclusive. Use them for your own information should you be asked a question(s) that you feel is offensive or illegal. Know ahead of time how you would answer it should the situation arise.

SUBJECT: NAME
Acceptable: "What is your full name?"
                    "Have you ever used an alias? If so, what was
                    the name you used?"
                    "What is the name of your parent or guard-
                    ian?" (Ask only if the applicant is a minor.)
Discriminatory: "What is your maiden name?" (Permissible
                    only for checking prior employment or edu-
                    cation.)
                    "Have you ever changed your name by court
                    order or other means?"

SUBJECT: RESIDENCE
Acceptable: "What is your address?"
                    "What is your telephone number?"
Discriminatory: "Do you rent or own your home?"
                    "Who resides with you?"
                    "How long have you lived in this country?"

SUBJECT: AGE
Acceptable: "Do you meet the minimum age require-
                    ment for work in this state?"
                    Statement that being hired is subject to ver-
                    ification that applicant meets legal age
                    requirements.
                    "If hired, can you show proof of age?"
                    "Are you over 18 years of age?"
                    "If under 18, after employment, can you
                    submit a work permit?"
Discriminatory: How old are you?
                    What is your date of birth?
                    Are you over the age of 40?

SUBJECT:	NATIONAL ORIGIN
Acceptable:	"Are you fluent in any languages other than English?" (You may ask this question only if it relates to the job for which the applicant is applying.)
Discriminatory:	Questions as to lineage, ancestry, national origin, nationality, descent, or parentage of applicant, applicant's parents, or spouse. "What is your mother tongue? What language do you commonly use?" "Dombrowski . . . that's Polish, isn't it?" "How did you acquire the ability to speak a foreign language?" "Where were you born?" "Are you a U.S. citizen?" "What is the citizenship of parents, spouse, or other relatives?" Requirement that applicant furnish naturalization papers or alien card prior to employment.

SUBJECT:	SEX, MARITAL STATUS, FAMILY
Acceptable:	Request for name and address of parent or guardian if applicant is a minor. Statement of company policy regarding work assignment of employees who are related.
Discriminatory:	"Are you male or female?" Questions about marital status. "Is that Miss or Mrs.?" "Are you married?" "What does your husband think about you working outside the home?" "Are you living with your spouse?" "Do you live with your parents?"

SUBJECT: RACE, COLOR
Acceptable: None.
Discriminatory: "What is your race?"
                Any questions regarding applicant's race,
                color, complexion, color of hair, eyes, or
                skin.

SUBJECT: PHYSICAL DESCRIPTION,
                PHOTOGRAPH
Acceptable: Statement that a photograph of the person
                may be taken after employment.
Discriminatory: Questions about an applicant's height and
                weight in the pre-employment interview.
                Request that an applicant affix a photograph
                to the application.
                Request for a photo after the interview but
                before employment.

SUBJECT: PHYSICAL CONDITION, DISABILITY
Acceptable: "Are you able to perform the essential func-
                tions of this job with or without reasonable
                accommodation?"
Discriminatory: Questions regarding applicant's general
                medical condition, state of health, or ill-
                nesses in the pre-employment interview.
                Questions regarding receipt of workers'
                compensation.

SUBJECT: RELIGION
Acceptable: Statement by employer of regular days,
                hours, or shifts to be worked and the expec-
                tations of regular attendance.
Discriminatory: "What is your religion?"
                "What church do you attend?"
                "What are your religious holidays?"

SUBJECT:	ARRESTS OR CONVICTIONS OF A CRIME
Acceptable:	"Have you ever been convicted of a felony?" (Such a question must be accompanied by a statement that a conviction will not necessarily disqualify applicant from employment.)
Discriminatory:	"Have you ever been arrested?"

SUBJECT:	BONDING
Acceptable:	Statement that bonding is a condition of hire.
Discriminatory:	Question regarding refusal or cancellation of bonding.

SUBJECT:	MILITARY SERVICE
Acceptable:	Questions regarding relevant skills acquired during applicant's U.S. military service.
Discriminatory:	General questions regarding military service such as date and type of discharge. Questions regarding service in a foreign military.

SUBJECT:	ECONOMIC STATUS
Acceptable:	None.
Discriminatory:	Questions regarding applicant's current or past assets, liabilities, or credit rating including bankruptcy or garnishment.

SUBJECT:	ORGANIZATIONS, ACTIVITIES
Acceptable:	"Please tell me about *job-related* organizations, clubs, professional societies, or other associations to which you belong. You may omit those that indicate your race, religion, creed, color, national origin, ancestry, sex, or age."
Discriminatory:	"Please tell me about all organizations, clubs, societies, and lodges to which you belong."

SUBJECT: CHILD CARE

Acceptable: "Do you know any reason why you might not be able to come to work on time every day?" (Acceptable only if the question is asked of every applicant, regardless of sex.)

Discriminatory: "How many children do you have?"
"Who takes care of your children while you are working?"
"How old are your children?"
"Do you plan to have children?"

SUBJECT: REFERENCES

Acceptable: "By whom were you referred for a position here?"
"Name persons willing to provide professional and/or character references for you."

Discriminatory: Questions of applicant's former employers or acquaintances that elicit information specifying the applicant's race, color, religion, creed, national origin, ancestry, sex, age, physical handicap or disability, medical condition, or marital status.

SUBJECT: IN CASE OF EMERGENCY

Acceptable: Name and address of *person* to be notified in case of accident or emergency.

Discriminatory: Name and address of *relative* to be notified in case of accident or emergency.

E Sample Interview Questions and Answers

You will want to be prepared for a variety of interview questions. The following questions and responses are offered as samples of some of the questions typically encountered in a job interview. Read them and ask yourself how you would respond. Some of the questions are tough and will require a lot of thought before answering. Practice before the interview. Know what you want to say and how you plan to present your strengths as well as your weaknesses. Prepare for each interview as if it were the one that will lead to the job offer of your choice.

General Questions

An interviewer may ask any number of general questions, but these are five of the most commonly asked questions:

1. Why do you want to work here?

As discussed in Myth #35, researching the company is a critical part of interview preparation. Your reply to this question should include several positive remarks about the company and conclude with the statement that you believe working for them would provide a work environment where you could do your best work.

Example: "I understand your company is #1 in this area in [whatever]. You have a reputation in the business community as a leader in [field] and are an employer with progressive views. I feel that my skills and experience in this field would benefit your company, and working for your company would allow me to make a meaningful contribution to your company by [doing what]."

2. *How have you benefited from your work with your present/last employer?*

With this question the interviewer is looking for information about your development in your profession. The interviewer may also use your response to help evaluate your potential for future growth. Use a past-and-present approach in your answer, and be sure to demonstrate professional growth as an employee.

Example: "When I started on my job, my supervisor monitored my work carefully and met with me almost daily. She usually went into great detail about what she expected me to accomplish and I had to briefly report on my progress at the end of each day. I also consulted with her about various aspects of each project. Although I did make mistakes early in the job, I used them as opportunities to learn. Now I work independently and only meet with my supervisor briefly at the end of each week to review the status of current projects. I feel confident about my work and my ability to make decisions. I believe that management also has confidence in my abilities and my judgment and demonstrates this by allowing me to work independently."

3. *How do you manage to get away for interviews when you are still employed?*

Keep your answer short and don't say anything that might cause you to appear dishonest, such as, "I told my supervisor I had a doctor's appointment." You may view this as a "little white lie," but the interviewer won't see it that way and may feel that if you lied to your present supervisor, you would lie to a new employer. Most employees can arrange time off for interviews by using vacation, personal leave, or compensatory time.

Examples: "I arranged to take one-half day of vacation" or "I am using a personal day."

4. *How did your previous employers treat you?*

This is not the time to explain that your employers didn't appreciate you, didn't pay you enough, wouldn't give you promotions, etc. Remarks like these can cause the interviewer to wonder not only why your employers didn't value you more highly, but also whether perhaps *you* are the problem, not your employers. Even if you're not ecstatic about your present/former employers, find something positive to say about them. (Be sure, however, it's something you can back up with an example if asked.)

Suppose, for example, your previous/current employer demanded more than you felt reasonable from an employee, paid an acceptable but not exceptional wage, and you and your supervisor had a civil but not very personal working relationship. You could truthfully reply as follows without criticizing your employer.

Example: "The company expected the best from their employees and treated them fairly in return. I had an acceptable working relationship with my immediate supervisor."

5. *Tell me about yourself.*
Do not start with, "Well, I was born...." The interviewer isn't looking for the story of your life. Usually he or she is looking for information about your work experience. You can respond by either (a) talking about your skills, work experience, and personal goals that relate to the job, or (b) asking the interviewer to clarify whether he or she is seeking personal or business information.

Examples: (a) "I've always been interested in the field of [xxxx], and majored in [xxxx] in college in order to pursue that interest as a career. I have enjoyed my five years at XYZ Corporation and learned a lot. However, I realize that in order to continue to grow in this field I need to move on to a larger organization, such as your company, that offers the opportunity for professional growth and career advancement." Or, (b) "Is there a particular area of my background in which you're interested?"

Entry Level (Recent Graduates)

Job seekers who are recent graduates may have some prior interviewing experience acquired when they applied for part-time or temporary/seasonal work while still in school. The interview process for full-time career positions will in most cases be a different experience. The key here is to practice for your interview. Doing well in an interview is something that you can learn with preparation and practice. You may want to use a taped, mock interview as one way to prepare.

6. What was your major? How did you choose it?

The first question is fairly straightforward. (The interviewer will usually follow it with another question, as illustrated above.) A short answer is usually appropriate here. The exception might be if you majored in a field very different from the job field in which you're applying. In that case, you will need to explain how you can apply the education in your major to the job in question. If you mention that you changed your major while in school, the interviewer will ask what prompted that decision. Be prepared to answer this question with a solid response. It's not necessary to mention that you changed your major unless you feel it has an impact on the job.

Example: "I majored in business administration. I chose that field based on my pre-college experience in the business world during my last 2 years in high school. My summer jobs during college reinforced my decision for this career field."

7. Do you feel you did your best in school? If not, why not? If yes, what motivated you?

This is another multiple-question situation. The interviewer isn't going to accept a "yes–no" answer here. A good response can be a plus, whether your initial answer is "Yes" or "No." Also, if your answer is that you didn't do your best, don't begin your answer with a blunt, "No." Begin with a general statement.

Example: "In looking back, I would have to answer honestly that I probably didn't do my best in school, at least in the first 2 years. I found the adjustment to being on my own at college, and the very different academic approach of college professors as compared to my high school teachers, difficult to adjust to initially. As a result, while I passed all my classes with average grades, I could have scored higher. During my junior and senior years, however, I can honestly say that I did my best and my grade point average reflected that change."

Example: "Yes, I do feel that I did my best in school. Although I enjoyed my college experience as much as any other student I also realized what an opportunity I had. My parents worked very hard to send me to college. I also was awarded several scholarships. In addition, I worked part-time jobs while in college. I wanted to get the most from the opportunity and enjoyed a real sense of accomplishment when I maintained a high grade-point average."

8. Did you ever fail a class? If yes, what was the reason?

Hopefully you'll be able to answer with a simple, "No." In the event you did fail a class, your goal is to present the failure as a growth experience. Give the facts, but don't bare your soul and don't blame your instructor. It's also usually not a good idea to say that you had a problem due to a "personal situation." If you have the unhappy experience of failing more than one class, consider using the earliest failure as your response. Remember that the interviewer may decide to check your academic references, so don't put yourself in a compromising position by lying.

Example: "Yes, I failed a [xxxx] class in my freshman year. At that time I hadn't developed the good study habits I needed to do well in my classes. I learned from that mistake, however, and realized the importance of applying myself to my studies instead of just trying to slide through my classes. I'm happy to say that I had to go through that unpleasant experience only once."

Example: "Yes, I failed a [xxxx] class in my junior year. I didn't give the class the attention it required and paid for my negligence with a failing grade. However, I did take the class again and passed with a B. As uncomfortable as it was, the situation did teach me to apply myself fully to the task at hand."

9. How has high school or college prepared you for the "real world"?

The interviewer may have a misconception that all recent graduates are "party people" or "immature." Your answer to this question can demonstrate that you don't fall into either one of those categories.

Example: "Fortunately, my teachers didn't accept excuses for being late to class or incomplete assignments. I learned the importance of being punctual and of completing my work on time. College also taught me to work independently and not to expect a teacher to push me to do the work. I learned that I would 'sink or swim' on my own. An additional benefit of college was the opportunity to meet a wide variety of people and learn more about how others viewed life."

10. I see you listed a number of part-time and summer jobs while you were in college. Which of these did you like the least? Why?

Many jobs, especially part-time or temporary jobs, contain a certain amount of boring work that's often repetitious. The interviewer's intent here is to find out what kind of attitude you had toward your jobs. As with many of the other questions, keep in mind that you want to give a positive answer.

Example: "Each of my jobs had its good and bad points. I tried to learn as much as possible at each job in order to gain experience and not let any negative parts of the job get in the way."

If the interviewer presses you to choose one particular job you disliked most and why, beware of telling him or her the job bored you.

Example: "I suppose job X would have to qualify for that designation because it offered the least opportunity for me to learn and increase my skills on the job."

When Changing Career Fields

If you are in the process of changing career fields, or perhaps changing to a different area within the same career field, you can expect the interviewer to probe a little more deeply into your reasons for the change and whether you're committed to your new career choice.

11. *What is your reason for the decision to make a job or career change*
    at this time?

Whatever your reason for making a career change, you want to present your decision as one made thoughtfully, and with every belief that you can succeed in your new field. Don't mention your age (e.g., "Well, if I don't make it while I'm still in my 50's, I won't do it."). Also, keep the answer fairly short.

Example: "Although I found satisfaction in my career initially, over the past few years I realized that this was no longer true. I made my career choice as an immature teenager. When I became interested in the field of [xxxx] about 2 years ago, I talked to a number of people whose opinions I respected about entering the field. Each of them encouraged me to make the change. I believe this change will ultimately benefit me both professionally and personally."

12. *Why do you feel you are qualified for this position?*

Before you answer, clarify whether the interviewer is looking for job-related qualifications or education-related qualifications, or both. Then address those concerns in your answer.

Example: "I've taken night courses at the community college for the past 18 months in [xxxx]. I also feel that there are many areas of my former profession, such as [xxxx], [xxxx], and [xxxx], where my skills and experience will easily transfer into this position."

13. *Do you feel you'll be able to cope with the change in environment? How? (or Why?)*

This is a question that's looking for your weaknesses; you have the opportunity to present a positive answer.

Example: "Life is a series of changes. This is just one more, but one that I look forward to making. It will be a challenge, but one that I find exciting. I'm confident that I'll make the transition successfully."

14. *How do you feel you can contribute to this organization?*

Other than the experience and skills listed on your resume, the interviewer wants to know what other assets you bring with you to the job.

Example: "In addition to my training and experience, I'm a very positive person, a hard worker, and someone who's interested in reaching for that higher level. Because I'm newer to the field than other employees, I'll work harder to prove myself and to attain the same level of expertise. Also, I believe that the fact that I'm new to this field allows me to bring a higher degree of enthusiasm to the job."

15. *Why do you think you would like this type of work?*

The goal of the interviewer with this question is to see whether you really understand what the specific job or profession involves, especially on a daily basis. Your pre-interview research on the company should help you here.

Example: "I've researched the field in general very carefully as well as spoken with people in similar jobs throughout the industry. I feel I have an excellent understanding of the 'pluses and minuses' where this type of work is concerned. I didn't learn anything about the work that caused me to eliminate it from consideration. This type of work is exciting because it presents a challenge."

Returning to the Business World

If you've decided to seek employment outside the home after being away from work for a number of years (e.g., mothers returning to the work force when their children enter school), you face a different set of circumstances than employed or just recently unemployed candidates. You have no immediate past job references, so the interviewer must try to determine your potential as an employee through questioning.

16. *What is your reason for deciding to return to the work force at this time?*

This is a logical question under the circumstances. However, the interviewer isn't interested only in your reason for returning but in how well you express that reason and present yourself. Avoid unprofessional remarks such as, "Well, with the kids gone all day I figured I might as well do something with myself." Or, "My husband recently retired and he's driving me crazy. I've got to get out of the house!" Also, if you're a mother returning to the work force, don't disparage your role as a homemaker. Give the interviewer a simple and professional answer.

Example: "When my children were born, I decided to stay home with them until the youngest was in school. Now that time has arrived. I enjoyed my work as an administrative assistant before I had the children, and I'm excited about returning to work."

17. *What have you been doing since you left your last job?*

The interviewer is looking for information about what you've done outside of the obvious (i.e., homemaking, child care, etc.). This gives you an opportunity to talk about any civic or charitable volunteer work you've done. If you've done any form of work at home, you can also mention it at this time.

Example: "In addition to raising my family, I enjoyed the opportunity to work with the women's league and was in charge of a very successful fundraiser for the local cub scout troop of which my son was a member."

Example: "During the time I spent at home I did volunteer work at the hospital and for two civic organizations. This gave me a chance to use my secretarial skills. I also typed papers for students at a nearby college, and I have a home computer which has allowed me to develop my computer skills."

18. What are your long-term employment goals?

The interviewer wants to determine whether you're committed to returning to the work force and resuming a career or just looking for something not too demanding that will bring in some extra income. Either reason is acceptable in itself, but the interviewer needs to know your goals in order to determine not only whether you're a good choice for the job, but whether the job is right for you.

Example: "I'm not sure about my long-term goals. At this time I know I definitely want to work outside the home, but I want to see how that goes before I make further plans."

Example: "My immediate goal is to obtain a job in my career field. I consider my return to work permanent, and my long-term goal is to become part of management."

19. What are your immediate employment goals?

As with question #18, the interviewer wants to determine how you view yourself and the return to work. Be realistic and honest.

Example: "My immediate goal is to find a part-time job that will allow me to re-enter the business world but also enable me to be home by the time my children return from school."

20. Would the fact that most of our employees are not your age bother you?

Although questions about age are illegal under federal law, interviewers may not feel that a question such as the above is inappropriate. They know that sometimes an older person returning to the work force may find it difficult to accept supervision from someone younger. They also want to gauge your reaction to this question. A simple statement will suffice for this question, but you can add an additional positive note to that statement if you wish.

Example: "The ages of the people I work with don't matter to me. I believe my maturity would be an asset to the organization, and I'm eager to learn and acquire new skills."

When Seeking Employment Due to Termination/Resignation

Whether you are interviewed after being terminated or after having resigned due to personal choice, you can expect the interviewer to probe the reasons for these circumstances. Your goals are to provide honest answers without telling more than is necessary and to present the situation in as positive a light as possible. If you lost a job due to downsizing or a company closing, the interviewer will understand that this was a situation beyond your control. If you were fired for cause, your answers to the interviewer's questions become even more important. If you resigned under pressure, or resigned due to personal choice, the interviewer will want to know why you made that decision. An interviewer may ask the following questions of any applicant, but an unemployed candidate can *definitely* expect these questions. If you are still employed but want to make a job change, the interviewer will also probe your reasons.

21. Have you ever been fired?

Although most of us would like to be able to always say "No" to this question, the facts of life are that some people would have to answer "Yes" in order to be truthful. If you have to answer in the affirmative, the interviewer's next question will in all likelihood be, *"Why were you fired?"*

Remember that many people have been fired. In fact, some organizations have a reputation for firing employees, especially management-level people. The fact that you were fired will not automatically eliminate you from consideration by an interviewer, but it will cause him or her to probe for additional data.

If you lost your previous job as part of a work force reduction, you can simply state this information. You might want to include the number of other people who also lost their jobs in the reduction.

Example: "I lost my job, along with 12 other people, when the company reduced the work force for economic reasons."

The more difficult answer is that of the person terminated for cause. Prepare a response that is honest but still puts you in as good a light as possible. Your goal is to demonstrate that you matured and learned from the experience. Misrepresenting the situation is inadvisable because at some point the truth will come out; most experienced interviewers are able to determine when an applicant is trying to falsify information. Also, lying about your situation could be grounds for dismissal later if you do get the job.

Example: "As much as I regret it, I must say 'yes' to your question. I made the mistake of allowing a personal problem to interfere with my job. Looking back, I realize that my work absences were too frequent and I allowed my preoccupation with the problem to decrease my effectiveness on the job. When I realized what had happened and how it impacted my job and life, I began to take measures to resolve the problem. Unfortunately, this occurred too late to save my job. However, I'm confident that this will not happen again. I learn from my mistakes. Also, my former supervisor can speak for the quality of my work."

22. Have you ever been asked to resign?

If you have been in a "resign or be fired" situation, you may feel your answer to this question has to be, "Yes." However, there is a technical aspect involved here. If an employer told you, "You can resign or we'll let you go," he or she gave you an option. Therefore, technically the employer could not in the future say that he or she asked you to resign. Asking an employee to resign is the same as firing and could result in a legal battle. Therefore you can answer "No" to this question. Or you can choose to answer a qualified "Yes."

Example: "I once was in a situation in which my new supervisor suggested that I might be happier working elsewhere. I agreed and resigned."

23. Why do you want to leave your current job? Or, Why did you resign from your previous job?

If you're job hunting because you're unhappy with your supervisor, co-workers, the job itself, the hours, the dress code, etc., don't share this with the interviewer. You need to present a reason for leaving that won't hurt your chances for getting a job offer. This could include lack of career advancement opportunities, inadequate wages, or lack of challenge in the work, among others. Maybe the company has moved to a new location and you're no longer willing to make a long commute. You may have a perfectly logical and acceptable reason, such as your employer plans to close and has advised employees to seek other employment. Keep your answer positive, whatever your circumstances.

Example: "I've worked for XYZ Corporation for 5 years. I started out in the mail room and now I'm assistant to the vice-president. However, that's as far as I'll be able to progress in the company, which is family-owned. I enjoy my job and have learned a great deal during my time with the company. However, in order to continue to advance in my field, I have to make a change."

24. What do you think is different between this job and the one you have now (or just resigned from)?

The research you did on the company before you came to the interview will help you with this question. The interviewer wants to determine why you think you'll be happier working for this company than your present/previous employer. He or she also wants to avoid hiring a difficult employee who may be changing jobs for petty reasons. Your answer should reflect positives about the prospective employer and your desire to grow as an employee, not belittle your present/former employer.

Example: "From what I've read about your company and the information I've gathered about this particular job, I feel I have the experience and drive to be successful in the position as well as be a contributor to the company. I believe one major difference in the jobs would be more opportunity to work independently once I have proven myself as an employee. I'm also attracted by the opportunity to advance my knowledge of the field through the employee training programs you offer."

25. How long have you been looking for a job?

The person who is job hunting while still employed has an advantage because the answer to this question isn't as important as answers to other questions. The interviewer understands that you're not going to give up a job unless you find a job that warrants the change. If you are unemployed, especially if you've been unemployed for a long time, then you want to include statements that can offset any negative impressions on the part of the interviewer.

Example: "It's been 2 years since I left my previous employment. During that time I have received several job offers, which I declined because I realized that in the long run they wouldn't be right for me. I view a job as too important to accept anything that comes along just to have something to do each day. I made a careful decision to wait for the right job and I still believe that's the best thing for me to do. I want to give my employer my best work and I believe that people who are unhappy in their jobs often find that hard to do."

Interviewing for a Temporary/Part-Time Position

Sometimes job seekers mistakenly think that an interview for a temporary or part-time position is not important simply because it's not for a "career" position. Although an interview for this type of job is often not as in-depth as an interview for an executive position, the prospective employer still wants to hire the best person for the job. Keep in mind, too, that temporary and part-time positions often result in offers of full-time, permanent employment. So think about what you can offer as a temporary or part-time employee that will make the interviewer choose you over the other candidates.

26. Are you looking for a permanent or temporary job?

There is an explanation for why an interviewer would ask this question when you've applied for a job advertised as temporary. First, the interviewer may want to make sure that you do understand the job is temporary. Second, the interviewer wants to know whether you're a person who really wants permanent employment or just applied for the temporary job as a "stop gap" measure. It costs employers money to hire and train new employees, even temporary ones. They're not anxious to have to replace a temporary employee halfway through the work assignment because that person left for a permanent job.

Example: "I'm definitely looking for a temporary job at this time. I plan to return to school in the fall."

Example: "I hope to find a permanent position eventually, but am seeking temporary employment at this time as an opportunity to gain work experience. If I get the job, I will definitely stay for the 3-month job period."

27.   What aspirations do you expect to satisfy by accepting this position?
Many people use part-time/temporary situations as an opportunity to learn more about their chosen field, even if indirectly. For example, an accounting student accepted a clerical position in the accounting department of a large firm in order to learn more about the field and typical working conditions. She had the opportunity to observe first-hand both the ups and downs of her chosen profession. Keep in mind also that many employers hire temporary workers as a way to find permanent employees.

Example: "I have always been interested in the field of accounting. I understand that this position is of a clerical nature, but I would hope to have the opportunity to get at least a small taste of what it's like to work in an accounting department. Even though I would be doing non-accounting work, I still consider it a step in the right direction."
Example (non-related field): "Although I'm interested in the field of accounting, at this time I still want to explore other possibilities. I feel that this job would give me that chance."

28.   What do you feel is a satisfactory attendance record?
Some people may feel that the part-time/temporary job is less important than a full-time job; therefore, being at work every day and on time isn't important. The interviewer wants to determine as much as possible that the prospective employee has a good work ethic and attitude toward the job. Your answer can be short, or you can add more information if you prefer.

Example: "Being here every day and on time."

Example: "I believe in being at work every day and on time. I won't call in 'sick' because I stayed out too late the night before, and I won't let you down and simply not show up. Since this is a part-time job, I'd expect to schedule any appointments, such as a doctor or dental appointment, outside of my work schedule if at all possible."

29.   I hired someone from your school twice before and it didn't work out. Why do you think it would be different with you?
Since the interviewer didn't tell you what the problems were with the prior employees, you may ask for more information. *"May I ask you exactly*

what problems you had with those people?" Then you can address the issues he or she raises. If you try to answer without this information, you really have no basis from which to approach the question. Depending on what the interviewer tells you, phrase your answer to address his or her concerns. (Also keep in mind that the other person may be testing you with this question to see how you respond.)

Example: "I can understand your concern that they [were always late, used foul language, loafed instead of worked, etc.]. I assure you that this is not true of the students I know. I have never behaved in that manner on any job, even as a teenager, and my references can tell you that I have always been a hard worker."

30. Is there any reason why you will not be able to get to and from this job and on time?
Part of your preparation for the interview would be to decide how you would get to work if you got the job. If you don't have an easy way to get to work, you need to decide how you will handle this before you go for the interview. Companies know that people with transportation problems are more likely to get discouraged and quit. Your goal is to assure them that you don't have this problem.

Example: "I have my own car and transportation is not a problem."

Example: "I have checked the bus schedules from my home to this location, and transportation will not be a problem."

Interviewing for Management Positions
People applying for a management position face a different type of interview than, for example, an entry-level person. A management position requires a higher degree of responsibility and initiative. Each person has their own management style, and the interviewer will try to determine through the questions whether your style would work in his or her company. The interviewer will also probe for information on how you handle relationships with staff members, how you reward good employees and how you manage problem employees.

31.   How do you meet a challenge?

The interviewer wants information about your problem-solving skills and your attitude toward a difficult situation. Once you've answered the question in general, the interviewer may then ask you for a specific example. Before you go to the interview, review your work experience and decide what information you want to use if this happens.

Example: "I believe in a quick response to a challenging situation. That doesn't mean I make a decision without gathering information, but I feel it's best to act as quickly as possible. The first thing I do is outline the problem. I then decide what I have to do to solve it and then decide how I will go about achieving that objective."

32.   What is your definition of a conducive work atmosphere?

This may seem like a simple question but it can also be a tricky one. What kind of work atmosphere already exists in that company? The best way to answer this question is a short, basic, and positive answer.

Example: "One where employees care about their work, understand the value of teamwork, and turn out a good product."

33.   Tell me about people that you hired in previous jobs. How did they work out; were they long-term employees?

The interviewer wants to get an idea of your ability to put together a good staff. The question can also reveal a candidate's personality problems, if for example the candidate admits that he or she had three assistants within a short period of time. Again, focus on the positive. However, if you had an employee who was less than desirable, you can mention this in order to avoid sounding "too good to be true" as long as you present a solution to the problem.

Example: "I was very fortunate in that the people I hired in my last job, and in fact the job before that, proved to be as good as they appeared during their interviews. Most of the people I hired at XYZ Corporation are still with the company. I did have one instance when a man I hired had a drinking problem. However, the company's employee assistance program helped him overcome this difficulty and although he eventually left to work elsewhere, he left on good terms with me and the rest of the staff."

34. ***Tell me about a time when you had to tell a staff member that you were dissatisfied with his or her work.***

Problem employees are a part of every organization. Sometimes even good employees on occasion produce less than satisfactory work. The interviewer wants insight into how you handle these situations, since this can partially determine your success as a manager.

Example: "First of all, I didn't wait too long to deal with the employee once I saw the problem. I didn't want her attitude and the fact that she wasn't carrying her share of the workload to destroy the morale of the rest of the staff. After a brief period of time in which I documented the problems and observed her relationships with the other employees, I spoke with her privately about the matter. She felt that her job description didn't cover the work required of her, so we went over the job description together item by item. Once she understood the job requirements, I shared with her my expectations for her as an employee and asked her if she wanted to continue with the company. She said that she did and is still with us today."

35. ***How do you reward people who work for you?***

Part of a manager's job is to motivate his or her employees about the work and their individual performances. While most companies have a system for performance evaluation and pay raises, what do you do to encourage and reward your employees over and above the customary? This is the time to tell the interviewer about innovative methods you use to inspire your employees.

Example: "First of all, I use a system that rewards not only the fast-trackers, but the slow and tenacious employees as well. I start by sharing my vision and communicate to them that we need to work together as a team to achieve that vision. Then I like to reward them when they least expect it. For example, my employees expect a Christmas bonus; it's traditional. However, when I send a gift basket, or a dinner certificate, or even a cash bonus to someone who's gone above and beyond the call of duty, I can see the excitement it generates. I also remember to reward my employees verbally and not take their hard work for granted. In addition, I try to reward them immediately for outstanding work instead of letting 6 months pass before I recognize their achievements."

Interviewing for Positions in Sales

High self-esteem is an important ingredient in the makeup of a successful sales associate. Salespeople need energy and the ability to communicate with all types of people. Furthermore, turnover is often high in this field. Interviewers want to weed out candidates not truly qualified to work in sales, especially among those candidates just entering the field.

36. *What qualifications do you have that make (or could make) you a successful salesperson?*

If you're an experienced salesperson, you know your qualifications and should have no problem stating them to the interviewer. Be sure to point out your successes with particularly difficult accounts. If you don't have a proven track record in sales, your answer needs to convince the interviewer that you could do the job.

Example: "I enjoy dealing with people and their different personalities on a daily basis. I also have a talent for persuading people to see things my way and the ability to convince them that what I'm offering is a good deal. I have the self-discipline that it takes to get up early on a cold, snowy day and go to work. I'm a self-starter and not easily discouraged when someone says 'no' to me."

37. *See this (pen, watch, cup, etc.) I'm holding; sell it to me.*

The interviewer may use this question to determine whether and how well you understand the basics of selling. It also gives the interviewer an opportunity to judge whether you can think on your feet. Include positive points about the item and its uses. Don't forget to close your remarks with a request for the order, just as you would if you were actually trying to make a sale. An experienced salesperson will likely have no problem with this question. If you're inexperienced in sales, consider the following illustration as a reply.

Example: "We're offering a new version of the familiar coffee cup today. This cup has several special features, including a thin drinking edge, an insulated cover to keep the contents warm, and a spread base to keep the cup from turning over if you place it on the dashboard of your car. It's available in ten different colors, has a 1-year guarantee against defects, and you can order this item in quantities of a dozen to the box. How many can I send you?"

38. How do you handle rejection?

If you're an experienced salesperson, you know that rejection is part of the job. If you're just entering the sales field and don't like the idea of a daily dose of rejection, you may want to reconsider your job choice. Accepting rejection is part of the salesperson's job; it goes with the business.

The interviewer asks this question as a way to determine whether you view a rejection by a potential customer as a rejection of the product or a personal rejection. Your goal is to let the interviewer know that you understand rejection is a part of the job and that it won't keep you from doing your work and doing it well.

Example (experienced): "I've been in sales for 5 years now and one thing I've learned is not to view rejection as a personal issue. Even if that customer doesn't want my product on a particular day, there's always the next prospect. And there's always the likelihood that the same customer who rejected me today will give me an order the next time I stop by. Each rejection just brings me that much closer to the customer who will say "yes.""

Example (inexperienced): "The sales field is new to me, but I've talked to many sales representatives and other people in the field. One thing I've learned from them is that rejection is part of the game. I'm not easily offended and I believe I have the ability to hear 'no' without being unduly upset by it."

39. What three things do you think are important to your success as a salesperson?

Most people would agree that a successful salesperson needs self-confidence, product knowledge, and the ability to shrug off rejection. Another important factor is customer knowledge; successful salespeople know their customers' needs before telling them what they've got to sell. Your answer can be short and to the point.

Example: "Having self-confidence, knowing my product, and knowing my customer."

40. How do you feel about cold calling?

For some salespeople, this is the least desirable part of the job. Since this is usually a part of a sales representative's responsibilities, the interviewer wants to hear you reassure him or her that you can handle the situation.

Example: "When I first entered sales, I dreaded cold calling. That was my weakest point. However, I enjoyed sales work so much that I decided I wasn't going to let it get me down. I decided to use a daily goal of a certain number of cold calls. Once I completed my goal for the day, I moved on to other parts of the job that I enjoyed more. The more calls I made, the easier it became to make them. Before long, I discovered that I accepted cold calling as just another part of the job. Today I feel very confident in this area."

Stress Interviews

Although most people would agree that every interview is stressful, some interviewers use the "stress method" of employing negative and trick questions to see how you react under pressure. The interviewer wants to determine who you "really are" when barraged by non-stock questions. Your goal is to remain calm, turn the questions to your advantage if possible, and avoid "foot in mouth" answers that can spell the end of your chances with that company.

41. *How do you feel about taking calculated risks when necessary?*
Before you attempt to answer this question, have the interviewer qualify the question. How does the interviewer define "calculated risks" and what kind of risks did he or she have in mind? You'll need to know more about the question before you can give an answer. Keep in mind that whatever your answer to this question, be sure to include the following.

Example: "Even if I determined that it was in the company's best financial interests to take such a risk, I would never take any sort of risk that put the safety of the company or its employees at stake. That includes the risk of jeopardizing my personal reputation or the company's reputation or the reputation of any employee. I don't think any employer would want an employee to take such a risk."

42. *Tell me, what is the worst thing you've heard concerning our company?*
This type of question can definitely catch you off guard, but if you've prepared for it in advance, it won't be hard to handle. Part of the impact comes from the question's implication that you have heard something bad about their company, which makes it a loaded question. However, if you had

heard bad things about the company, it's unlikely that you would be there applying for a job. The interviewer knows this and does not expect you to say negative things about the business. (Don't be naive enough to think you're actually expected to make a negative remark about the company.) Smile and be pleasant but let your answer show the question didn't intimidate you.

Example: "You have a reputation for being tough to get a job with, but you also have a reputation for hiring only the best."

43. I'd like to hear about a situation where you put your foot in your mouth.

Everyone puts their foot in their mouth at one time or another in life. That doesn't mean you have to share your worst experience with the interviewer. And you don't have to automatically use an experience that occurred in the workplace. Answer the question with an illustration that's truthful but humorous, and end by commenting that you learned a lesson from the incident.

Example: "Several years ago I made a joke about an ugly pair of shoes in a store window only to discover that the friend I was with had purchased an identical pair the previous day. Fortunately my friend took it as a joke and we've laughed over it many times since then. Despite my embarrassment, however, it did teach me to 'look before I speak' and made me more aware of what I say socially and in the workplace."

44. How would you evaluate me as an interviewer?

Experienced job seekers will know better than to take this question as an honest invitation to tell the interviewer what you think; novice job seekers need to learn that too, and quickly. Even if you didn't like the interviewer, thought he or she did a terrible job and shouldn't be interviewing people at all, don't yield to the temptation to express your opinion, despite the interviewer's smile which seems to invite your candid response. You also don't want to appear too "gushy" even if you felt the interviewer was a great person who did a good job. That's not what the question is really about. Answer carefully.

Example: "This has been an interesting interview. You were very thorough in your questioning. I also understand that you've tried to give me a feeling for what the job pressure would be like, and you're obviously very determined to find the right person for the position. Speaking along that line, how do you think I fit your idea of the person you want for the job?"

45.   *What two questions do you not want me to ask?*
This is another loaded question. Again, be careful of your answer. One tactic would be to reply with a totally unimportant question, such as, "I'm glad you didn't ask me for the address of my college." However, you don't want to appear flippant. Another response would be to declare that there aren't any questions you don't want the interviewer to ask.

Example: "I honestly can't think of anything along that line. I like to think of myself as an honest person who's not afraid to answer any question related to the job or my qualifications for the job. I do appreciate your professionalism in not asking me illegal or inappropriate personal questions."

Job-Related Travel

In view of the amount of travel involved in today's business environment, an interviewer will very likely ask questions to determine whether there is potential for problems with job-related travel. Your goal is to answer without over-committing yourself one way or the other. You also don't want to stop the interview with an adamant answer that doesn't leave any room for negotiation.

46.   *How much travel did your previous job require?*
The interviewer may use this question to determine whether you'd be a good fit for a job that required travel or perhaps unhappy in a new job that didn't require travel. You need to phrase your answer to demonstrate that you're open to different degrees of travel.

Example: "My previous job required me to travel only once a month for 2 or 3 days at a time. I enjoyed traveling and would welcome the opportunity to travel more in performing my job duties."

Example: "My previous job required me to travel extensively. Although I had no problem with that, I also have no problem with traveling less."

47. How much job-related travel is too much?

If you're willing to travel extensively, this is your opportunity to say so. If you're not, then you need to phrase your answer accordingly.

Example: "I don't think there's any amount of travel that I would consider too much. I enjoy traveling and have no problems with being away from home for extended periods of time."

Example: "I don't mind job-related travel, but I'd like to know more about the specific amount of travel you have in mind."

48. How do you feel about traveling? Would you be willing to go where the company sends you?

This is a mixed question. Is the interviewer asking you whether you're willing to relocate, be out of town all week every week, or travel occasionally? Perhaps it's just a curiosity question; the job doesn't require any travel or relocation, but the interviewer wondered what you'd say. First, get more information. Answer the question with a question (see below). Otherwise the best answers would be, "Fine" and "Yes." If you say "No" it could immediately remove you from consideration. If you progress to the point where you receive a job offer and decide at that time that you're unwilling to travel, you can always decline the job offer or perhaps negotiate the amount of travel.

Example: "Do you mean business travel, or are you speaking in terms of relocating?"

49. What difficulties does traveling present for you?

Sometimes people get jobs, then discover that travel is a problem. Somewhere along the process, the communication didn't include the information that the position involved a lot of travel time. Difficulties could include family objections to time away from home, your personal objection to being away from home, or a physical condition you have that makes traveling difficult. (Hopefully you won't apply for a job that involves extensive traveling if it will present difficulties.) It is discriminatory for an interviewer to ask questions about an applicant's general medical condition, state of health, or illnesses in the pre-employment interview, but it is not illegal to ask about problems with traveling. This is an opportunity for you to determine the amount of travel involved in the position. Ask for more information if you truly have reservations about travel. Otherwise use a simple response.

Example: "Travel is not a problem."

50. What do you consider a benefit of traveling other than accomplishing your work goals?

This question provides an opportunity to indicate your interest in growing within the company, your willingness to be a team player, and your interest in growing professionally as an individual.

Example: "Obviously the number one purpose of the travel would be to fulfill my job requirements. However, I would enjoy the opportunity to visit branch offices and meet other company employees. The travel could also give me the benefit of learning more about the areas I traveled to and I could quite possibly use this information for future projects."

Attitude

Attitude is an individual's point of view or way of looking at things. It's also readiness to react in a pre-determined manner. The interviewer looks for people with positive outlooks, those who don't dwell on misfortunes. Negative attitudes, like positive ones, are contagious. The interviewer wants to know how well you can get along with others and about your willingness to cooperate.

With regard to your attitude during the interview, don't insult the interviewer. Even if you think he or she is incompetent, back off. Remember, whatever your opinion of the interviewer, that individual decides whether or not you move to the next stage of the interview process. You may be smarter than the interviewer, but he or she is the one making the decision concerning your future with the company.

51. What does your immediate supervisor do that you dislike?

Don't tell the interviewer what your supervisor does that you dislike. He or she is testing both your attitude and your loyalty with this question. Just make a general statement about how you view your relationship.

Example: "My relationship with my supervisor is professional and I don't think of it in terms of like or dislike. We work together as a team to get the job done."

52. *Do you prefer to work alone or as part of a team?*

This is another question where it's important for you to have an understanding of the job before you answer, then phrase your answer accordingly. Usually the interviewer asks this question to determine whether or not you're a team player. However, suppose the job you've applied for is one where you would work alone the majority of the time? The interviewer may not rate "team player" as important as "doesn't mind working alone." The safest reply is a neutral one.

Example: "I'm equally happy working alone or as part of a team."

53. *Would you have difficulty working with people whose backgrounds and interests are different from your own?*

This is another "team player" type question. If you say "Yes" then the interviewer will probe into how you feel and why. The best answer is a simple one.

Example: "No, I wouldn't have difficulty working with people of different backgrounds and interests from mine. I enjoy working with a diverse group of people."

54. *Why are you interested in this job?*

The purpose of this question is to separate the candidates with a sincere interest in the position from those who just want a job—any job. This also helps the interviewer to identify a candidate's career ambitions and whether those ambitions are consistent with the position. Your responsibility here is to demonstrate that you've done your homework in learning about the company and are able to communicate to the interviewer specifics about your interest in the position.

Example: "I've been aware of your company's growth over the past few years and I've studied information about department X in particular. I'm very interested in [area] and feel that my academic background and previous work experience, particularly in the area of [xxxx], would enable me to make a significant contribution to your company. This job would also offer me an opportunity for professional growth and advancement."

55. What is your definition of cooperation?

This is another team player question. The interviewer wants to know how you will function in the workplace.

Example: "To me cooperation means putting personal desires and beliefs aside in order to help the department and/or the company reach its goals."

Work Experience

The interviewer uses questions regarding work experience to help him or her look for information about what candidates did in previous jobs and how well they did it. He or she also wants to see how you progressed in previous jobs.

56. What do you feel you've learned from previous jobs?

The interviewer isn't looking for a list of things you learned to do on the job. He or she wants to know whether you accept and use constructive criticism/advice, and whether your personal preferences are more important to you than those of the company.

Example: "Although I've learned a variety of practical things, the most significant thing I've learned from my jobs is the importance of teamwork and cooperation. If the company does well, I do well. I've learned also that when my supervisor offers advice, it's to help me, not hinder me."

57. Tell me about your (or one of your) biggest accomplishments.

Remember to keep your answer related to what you've accomplished on the job. A number of projects should quickly come to mind, based on the work you did in preparing your resume. Don't exaggerate; if the interviewer asks for details, your exaggerated claims will quickly surface. If you have a major accomplishment outside the office related to the company's position in the community, you may wish to include that in your remarks.

Example: "I experienced a lot of satisfaction with the Renco Project and the way my team responded in dealing with the demands it placed upon us. I'm also proud of [other items] and the fact that all the projects came in on time and within the budget. I also enjoyed a sense of accomplishment when I chaired a company committee to raise money for the local hospital and we exceeded our goal by 35%."

58. How much experience do you have?
Your initial reaction here may be to impress the interviewer with as much experience as possible. Keep in mind, however, that you don't want to lose the job opportunity by appearing to have too much experience. Ask the interviewer to be a little more specific (e.g., *"Do you mean overall experience or experience in a specific area?"*). This also gives you an opportunity to think about your reply so that you can give an appropriate response. Although your reply will depend somewhat on the information you get from the interviewer, here are examples of two responses.

Example: "I have 7 years of experience as an accountant, with 5 of those spent in the tax department of XYZ Corporation. For the last 3 years I've served as supervisor of that department."

Example: "I have a variety of experience in a number of different areas of accounting. This has given me the experience to deal with a wide range of issues in the field. I've also had extensive supervisory experience in my present position."

59. What is your boss's title and what are his or her functions?
Why in the world would the interviewer ask you about your boss? The interviewer has a two-fold purpose for this question. One, if a candidate doesn't know his current boss's title and responsibilities, it shows a lack of depth and of interest in the company. Two, by knowing what the candidate's boss did, the interviewer can detect areas where the candidate might try to embellish his or her own responsibility or authority. This doesn't have to be a long answer. If the interviewer wants more information, he or she will ask.

Example: "My boss is Assistant Manager of XXXX Department, supervises 10 employees, and has responsibility for [name two or three main areas]."

60. Please tell me in as much detail as you can.... Here the interviewer asks you for detailed information about a particular procedure involved in your job.
This is one question where the interviewer does want detailed information about something specific. If you can't give it, the interviewer will know that you don't have the experience you claimed. The point here is not to list on your application experience you don't have.

Example: "First, I write in.... Next, I.... Then I.... Finally I...."

Handling Conflict

As nice as it would be to have a conflict-free workplace, the truth is that people do have conflicts, both personal and professional, on the job. The information the interviewer wants is how, and how well, you handle conflict in the workplace.

61. *Do you, or have you ever, experienced difficulty getting along with others?*

With this closed-ended question, the interviewer hopes to determine how well you interact with others. Are you someone who will disrupt the work of team members within the department, or are you willing to be a team player? The best response here is usually a simple "Yes" or "No." If you answer "Yes," and the interviewer probes for details, respond in as positive a light as possible.

Example: "Basically the only time I experienced a problem getting along with a fellow employee occurred when that person was habitually late with his portion of the project work, which delayed my work on the project. However, the department supervisor quickly recognized the problem and corrected the matter; my relationship with the other employee has been satisfactory since that time."

62. *Have you successfully worked with a difficult person?*

You may or may not have encountered a difficult person in the workplace. Most experienced employees have encountered such a person at one time or another. If you respond in the affirmative, the interviewer will likely ask you how you worked successfully with that person.

Example: "No, I've enjoyed working with my fellow employees and don't recall anyone I'd classify as difficult to work with."

Example: "Yes, I have." (After next question) "I once had to work with a person who resented the heavy workload we had at that time and had no qualms about verbalizing her dissatisfaction at every opportunity. I finally had a private talk with her, and told her as nicely as I could that her constant harping on the subject disturbed me. I suggested that we use our energy to get the work done rather than complain about it. After that she did her job without comment when we worked together, although I think she may have continued to annoy some of the other employees."

63. Tell me about a time when you had to take disciplinary action with someone you supervised.

Your answer here will tell the interviewer whether you're an "act before you think" person or someone who understands how to discipline an employee fairly and productively.

Example: "I once received an anonymous complaint about an employee. Although I had some concern over the method the person used to complain, the nature of the complaint indicated I needed to investigate. The first thing I did was to make sure I had all the facts. I reviewed work sheets, time sheets, and project records and also observed the individual in question over a period of about a week. At that time I felt the complaint was justified. I scheduled a private meeting with the employee to discuss the matter. First I asked the person if he was aware he was breaking the rules and allowed him to give me his version of what had transpired. Then I asked him to suggest a solution to the problem. As it turned out, I found his solution acceptable. However, due to the nature of the problem I did have to take disciplinary action, which involved putting a written memorandum of the proceedings in his personnel file. I also explained to him that we would review the matter again in 3 months and if there had been no further problems, this would also be noted in his personnel file. The employee, although upset over the written reprimand, thanked me for giving him the opportunity to correct the situation. He is still with my department today."

64. Tell me about the last time you lost your temper at work.

This is not the time for true confessions. If you feel you must admit to losing your temper, be sure to include a positive note.

Example: "I don't lose my temper at work."

Example: "I try not to lose my temper at work. If I occasionally become upset or annoyed, I go into my office, close the door, and ask my secretary not to disturb me for 10 minutes."

65. Tell me about a time when you and your boss disagreed, but you still found a way to get your point across.

You can either say that you've never had a disagreement with your boss, or you can offer a situation that puts both of you in a positive light.

Example: "I don't feel that my boss and I have disagreements. He welcomes my input, and I feel free to speak to him about all matters in the office. If he decides not to accept my suggestion, I view that as his prerogative as the department supervisor."

Problem-Solving Skills

Tackling problems is a tough job for most people. The interviewer wants to know whether you have the basic intelligence, common sense, and maturity to solve problems and make decisions.

66. *What would you do if you had to make a decision during a supervisor's absence and no procedure existed?*

The interviewer may use this question to determine your skills at analyzing a situation and your dedication to the company. He or she may also be probing for your loyalty to your manager.

Example: "If it was an urgent situation that had to have a decision when my manager wasn't available, I'd review all of the information I had and then make a decision based on that information. I would advise my supervisor of the situation and my actions at the very earliest opportunity."

67. *What steps do you take to solve a problem?*

The interviewer isn't talking about merely deciding on the next step in a project. When something goes wrong, what do you do? Most solutions involve an analysis of the problem and then a logical sequence of steps to correct the problem.

Example: "First, I find out why things have gone wrong. What caused the problem? If there's more than one part to the problem, I prioritize the parts and tackle the most difficult one first. I look below the surface to be sure I know the real cause of the problem, then analyze the situation in order to determine who or what is responsible. The next step is to decide how I'm going to handle it, and the final step is to take the corrective action."

68. *How long does it typically take you to make a decision?*

The interviewer isn't looking just for a length of time with this question. Your answer will also tell him or her whether you tend to make snap decisions or weigh matters carefully first. Since the amount of time you spend on a decision may vary according to the problem, say so.

Example: "That would depend on the situation and the type of decision I had to make."

If the interviewer probes for a more exact answer, you still don't have to answer in terms of minutes or hours.

Example: "If it's a fairly routine decision that I've made often before, I'd probably make it in a matter of minutes. If it's an involved situation that needs investigation, it could take me anywhere from several hours to several days to make a decision. I feel the important thing is that I make the right decision rather than an incorrect hasty decision."

69. How do you enlist the help of others in solving a problem?

If you say that you never enlist the help of others, this could identify you as a "loner." Most employers value team efforts. With this question, the interviewer will try to determine whether you order others to help or get their assistance agreeably.

Example: "When a problem presents itself that I feel warrants the attention of either a team in the department, or perhaps the entire department, I call together the people I feel are best qualified to work on the problem. First I state the problem clearly and tell them that I want their assistance in finding a solution. I emphasize that I value everyone's input. We make a list of all possible causes, and then select the most likely cause. After that we brainstorm for solutions and then evaluate each proposed solution. We consider each person's suggestion and don't judge any idea as "unacceptable" until the group has discussed its merits. Then we choose the best solution and develop an action plan. Finally, I thank each of them for their time and input and the satisfactory resolution of the problem."

70. Tell me about an unconventional method you have used to solve problems.

Before you go to the interview, think back over how you have handled problems in your department. If you don't use any unconventional methods, it's best to say so. If you do, then offer that information.

Example: "To date the conventional problem-solving methods have worked fine in our department. This doesn't mean I wouldn't consider using an unconventional method if the occasion arose."

Example: "We use 'rolestorming' in our department. It's a combination of brainstorming and role-playing. Each person takes on the role of someone who's not present and then for about 20 minutes brainstorms ideas from the other person's perspective."

Leadership Skills

The most important relationship in the work setting is between the employee and the person to whom the employee will report. The interviewer will take particular care when screening for leadership positions. If the company hires someone difficult to work with, out of step or at odds with the organization's culture, it can mean trouble.

71. *How do you go about delegating?*
Effective leaders know how to delegate and recognize its importance. Delegating allows others to grow in handling responsibility. It also frees the manager's time for more critical matters. Leaders who refuse to delegate can waste enormous amounts of time doing work that their employees could easily handle. Reluctance to delegate can also indicate a need on the leader's part to control everything and everyone and keep his or her leadership position secure. The interviewer's questions will help to identify those who hesitate to delegate as well as those who know how to delegate and do it well.

Example: "I prefer not to delegate. If you want something done right do it yourself is my motto." *(Not a good answer.)*

Example: "First I know the individual talents of each person in my department and their particular skills. I don't delegate work to someone who I think won't be successful. I'm also very specific with my employees about how much authority I'm giving them. We establish controls, such as budgets, deadlines, and periodic reviews. I also give employees a way to measure their own success so that they'll know when they've done a good job. Each morning we hold a very brief meeting at which each person gives me a one- or two-sentence update. If we need to discuss a particular matter, we set aside a separate time to do that later in the day. I let my employees know when they've done well and help them learn from their mistakes. As an employee grows in his or her job, I delegate more."

72. Describe your leadership role.

Effective leaders know how to delegate, manage a meeting, gain cooperation, and resolve conflict. By asking you to describe your leadership role, the interviewer can determine whether you lead or push, encourage or dictate, work beside your employees or stand apart.

Example: "I believe that a manager's responsibility goes beyond attending meetings, preparing budgets, and solving problems. I believe that my role is to build and maintain a motivated team. This takes patience, energy, and know-how as well as the willingness to work with my staff. I'm willing to listen to what my people have to say, but I make the final decision on critical matters."

73. What makes you an effective leader?

A continuation of question #72. Now that you've told the interviewer how you lead, he or she wants to know how that makes you effective.

Example: "I believe in teaching others rather than doing everything myself. I try to implement methods that make their jobs interesting; I keep everyone informed about what's happening in the department and in the company. I never ask an employee to do something I wouldn't be willing to do myself. I stand behind my employees. If an employee needs critical feedback, I hold the meeting privately at the end of the day. I work hard and expect my employees to do the same, but I let them know that I appreciate their efforts."

74. Would you describe yourself as a natural born leader?

This can be a tricky question. You want to sound confident but not cocky. How the interviewer perceives your answer also depends on what he or she considers a "natural born leader." Your answer will depend to some extent on the position for which you're interviewing.

Example: "Since the definition of a 'natural born leader' could vary from one person to another, I'd prefer to say that I have worked hard to develop any leadership skills that I have and to acquire those that I didn't have."

75. How do you offer criticism to employees?

Criticism is difficult for most people to take and it's also not easy to give. Often it's not what someone says, but how they say it that counts. Obviously anyone in a leadership position will have to offer an employee constructive criticism at some point. The interviewer wants to know whether your goal is to embarrass your employees or encourage them.

Example: "I believe in giving criticism in a positive manner as a way of helping the employee change. I do not use the 'sandwich technique' of inserting my critical comments between beginning and ending words of praise. I feel that doing so can confuse some employees. I believe in presenting the problem area to employees, giving them time to offer any information they feel is relevant, then lay out for them the corrective action that they need to take. I always end by letting them know that I want them to grow professionally and be a successful employee."

Initiative

You can't teach someone to have initiative, a trait that most companies value highly in employees. The interviewer wants to see whether you, the candidate, has enough initiative to meet the needs of the position. Are you a self-starter or do you need a lot of encouragement to get the job done? The interviewer's questions search for this information.

76. What have you done that shows initiative?

Are you a doer—someone who on their own looks for ways to improve efficiency or sales, save money or time—in general the kind of person who makes things easier for their manager and their co-workers? That's what this question is asking.

Example: "I like to anticipate my supervisor's needs and have things ready before she asks for them. Before I go to her with a request, I always get my data and facts together and have the information in a report ready to hand to her along with the request. I also look ahead to future needs and plan my work accordingly. I like to find ways to save time and money. One example is a form I designed recently to track statistics on a daily basis."

77. How do you organize and plan for major projects?

Effective planning requires that the person be able to see the whole picture and plan for the work in a way that will meet the necessary completion date. Many people don't plan at all; they just do whatever seems most pressing at the moment. The interviewer can determine from your answer whether you have organizational skills.

Example: "First I determine the date the job must be completed. Then I break down the work into weekly components, allowing extra time for the unexpected. I decide who will work on the project and assign their area of responsibility. I also do a budget review to make sure we'll be able to complete the project within the allotted budget."

78. How do you go about setting goals?

Researchers have found that most peak performers are obsessive goal-setters motivated by compelling, burning, internal drive. Goal-setting has a critical impact on your attitude. The interviewer wants to know whether you're a realistic goal-setter or someone who has only vague goals with no real idea of what you want to accomplish.

Example: "I set realistic goals that are clearly defined, specific, and measurable. I write these goals down and state them in a positive way. Because I realize that sometimes goals have to be flexible, I continually update my goals to meet changing needs. I always have a deadline in mind. One thing that helps me attain my goals is to visualize what I plan to accomplish and the benefits it will bring."

79. On a scale of 1 to 10, on average, where is your energy level?

Although you may feel confident saying "10," the interviewer will probably press you for an example. One way to handle this is to describe a typical day that demonstrates good use of your time. You want to emphasize that you give your all to the job.

Example: "At the end of the day I don't leave until I've prepared my list of objectives for the next day and returned all of my phone calls. I believe on average, my energy level is an 8 or 9."

80. Tell me something you did that demonstrates your willingness to work hard.

This is an opportunity for you to share an experience in which you perhaps handled an unexpected problem, or anticipated a problem, and worked on your own to overcome it.

Example: "Our office seemed to always get started late because one of the machines used by the technician had to warm up before she could use it. Since she didn't arrive until the last moment each morning, by the time she turned on the machine and it was ready, we were already 15 minutes behind schedule. One day I asked her to show me how to turn on the machine. It was a simple procedure that anyone could do. Since I arrived at the office a half-hour earlier than the others, I volunteered to turn on the machine first thing in the morning. By the time the technician arrived, the machine was ready and we could start our appointments on time each day."

Qualifications

You have enthusiasm, initiative, desire to succeed, willingness to work, a great personality, you're a team person but you don't mind working alone—does all of this qualify you for the job of your dreams? No, not if you don't have the necessary education, training, and experience.

81. Do you have a degree?

Depending on whether a company requires a degree to consider you as a candidate and on whether or not you have a degree, your answer could eliminate you from consideration. If the position requires a degree and you don't have one, your job is to sell yourself to the interviewer as someone whose experience more than compensates for the lack of a degree. If you're able to do this the lack of a degree may not ruin your chances. If you have a degree, then say "Yes." Do not elaborate until you have more information. Once you know what the interviewer is looking for you can provide information that speaks to that need.

Example: "Yes, I have a degree. What are you ideally looking for?"

Example: "I don't have a formal degree at this time because I had to leave college after my junior year due to my father's death. However, I believe that my experiences in life and work are assets that give me value to a company. I also plan to continue my education in the evening and obtain my degree within the next 2 years."

82. What are some of the reasons you've been successful in your profession?

The interviewer is looking for information about what makes you who you are more than specific examples of your success. A short answer will be sufficient here.

Example: "I believe my success is due to my determination to find solutions to problems, to find a way to accomplish my goals even if it means many hours of hard work, and my belief in myself as a person who can achieve my goals."

83. How would you proceed to install a (system applicable to the position)?

Candidates sometimes claim qualifications that they don't have. Many interviewers will use a question such as this to determine whether a candidate has the basic technical knowledge to meet the job requirements. In this instance, as in question #60, the interviewer wants a detailed explanation that will demonstrate your qualifications for the job.

Example: "First I would...., then...., then.... I'd finish the installation by...."

84. What can you do for us that someone else cannot do?

By the time the interviewer asks this question, you should have received a full explanation of the job for which you're interviewing. If that hasn't occurred, you will need to ask questions to get that information. Then respond by using a recap of the job description, adding what you personally can bring to the job, e.g., your determination, your analytical skills, etc.

Example: "I can perform all of the requirements of the job description as we've discussed them. However, in addition I feel that I can give you some fresh perspectives on [area] due to my background in [area]. I also believe I have a firmer grasp of the [area] procedures than many people in my profession, and could apply that knowledge to this position."

85.   *What are your qualifications?*
Don't rattle off a string of degrees, or detailed lists of training and work experiences. This information is on your resume. Give a thorough but brief statement about why you're qualified for the job.

Example: "I have my master's degree in business administration, have worked in this profession from the ground floor up to a supervisory level at my present position, and have an excellent work record at both my present position and prior jobs. I have acquired specialized skills in [area] and update my knowledge of the field periodically through continuing education classes. I believe that my varied and extensive background in this field qualifies me for this position."

Decision-Making Skills

Many people find it difficult to make decisions. Some people can make decisions but do not enjoy doing so; they are excellent and dependable workers who simply prefer that others make the decisions. Then there are people who want to make decisions but don't necessarily make good ones. The interviewer's job is to determine whether you possess any decision-making skills necessary for the position.

86.   *What criteria do you use to make decisions?*
If you have limited decision-making experience in your previous jobs, think about how your supervisors made decisions. What criteria do you think they used? Did you feel comfortable with their decision-making? If so, you can use that as your basis for your answer. If you have decision-making experience, then you can reply with your own criteria.

Example: "That the decision is one that will be good for the employee, the department, and the company; that it is a workable decision; and that it is one that I personally believe is right for the situation."

87.   *Give me two examples of decisions you had to make on your last job.*
Be careful in choosing your examples; don't give anything too weak or too extreme.

Example: "I had to determine each month whether to authorize the over-time for certain projects. This required considering the status of a project, the amount of overtime requested, and whether the work accomplished would justify the costs. Sometimes I had to say 'no'. I also had to make a decision once about terminating an employee who had been with the company for quite some time. Unfortunately, as difficult as it was, I determined that the employee's behavior was putting the company at risk and so I did terminate his employment."

88. Tell me about a time when you had to make an unpopular decision.

The interviewer wants to know that you would be willing and have the strength to make an unpopular decision. You don't have to give an example that sounds like an uprising, but do use an example that presents you as a strong person willing to do what is best for the company.

Example: "We traditionally gave our employees a half-day off during the community festival time. This was something the company had done for a number of years, but was not a specified employee benefit. Last year, due to a breakdown in the machinery earlier in the month, we were so far behind on our orders that I made a decision not to give the employees the festival day. I understood their disappointment, but when I weighed the possibility of losing orders and customers against the disappointment of the employees, I decided in favor of filling the orders and making our customers happy. Without customers, our employees wouldn't have jobs. I notified the employees well in advance so they wouldn't be disappointed at the last minute."

89. What kind of decisions are most difficult for you?

Don't list major professional decisions as the most difficult. You don't want to appear weak or hesitant about making important decisions. Use an example that shows your sensitivity to human needs.

Example: "I believe most people would agree that making the decision to terminate an employee is one of the most difficult decisions a manager has to make. Other than that, I don't have too much difficulty with making decisions. I usually know what has to be done and I do it."

90. What type of decisions did you make on your last job?

Your answer here of course will depend on the decisions you made in your last job. If you didn't make decisions, say so.

Example: "I regard most of the decisions I made on my last job as the routine kind employees make on a daily basis. However, my supervisor often spoke with me at length about how he made decisions and taught me the importance of making good decisions."

Example: "I made decisions about hiring and firing for my department, approved the employee vacation schedule, assigned priority to the work, and scheduled projects for the department, plus the many other daily decisions made by managers everywhere."

Future Plans/Aspirations Regarding Employment

Part of what makes a candidate attractive to an interviewer is evidence that the candidate knows what they want and how they plan to go about obtaining it. Most interviewers are not impressed by someone who doesn't know what they want to do or what they hope to achieve in the future.

91. *What would you like to be doing 5 years from now?*

The interviewer may use this question as a starting point to explore your goals, how you selected them and why. It gives you the opportunity to demonstrate that you've given thought to your future and aren't just drifting along, although obviously you don't want to appear so rigid that you dis-qualify yourself from consideration. It also provides the chance to promote yourself as a team player and a professional. This is another instance where doing your research on the company before the interview pays dividends. If you're still somewhat uncertain about your long-range goals, be sure you have a clear picture of what motivates you at this time.

Example: "I feel very confident about what I want to do in my profession. I want to continue to develop my skills and be ready for a supervisory position by the end of next year, and a candidate for management within the next 2 or 3 years. I believe that I have the ability and drive to progress into an upper-level management position within the next 5 years."

Example: "I know definitely that I want to be in the field of [whatever]. At this point I'm still open to exploring the different areas in that field. Whichever area I choose to pursue, however, my goal is a management position within the next 5 years."

92. If you joined our organization, how long do you think you would stay?

This question may indicate that the interviewer considers you a candidate for a job offer. However, this is a tricky question and the answer is not a set time such as "2 years at most." You want to put the question back in the interviewer's lap with your answer.

Example: "I want a company in which I can settle down, and I believe your company offers that possibility. As long as I can grow professionally, I would have no reason to make a move. How long do you think this job would challenge me?"

93. If you joined our company, when would you expect a promotion?

The interviewer does not expect you to give a specific reply (e.g., "6 months"). Be careful in answering this question. You want to demonstrate that you have faith in yourself and your potential but are realistic enough to know that you have to earn a promotion.

Example: "My answer to that would depend on your company's criteria for promotion. I would not expect to be promoted without demonstrating my worth to the company and professional growth. However, I am looking for a company that believes in promoting from within and will encourage me to learn."

94. What are you looking for in your next job?

Don't tell the interviewer what you expect to get from the company. Instead, express yourself in terms of what you could give to an employer.

Example: "During my time at XYZ Corporation, I discovered a talent for training and motivating floor sales personnel, as demonstrated by the steady increase in sales each month. I want the opportunity to continue that sort of contribution in a company that encourages employee growth and with a supervisor who will help me develop professionally."

95. What criteria are you using to evaluate the company for which you want to work?

Unless you started applying for jobs and accepting interview appointments helter-skelter without any thought about finding the "right" job, you should have an idea of what you want in an employer. You can share this with the interviewer in a straightforward and simple answer. However, be aware of the status of the company for which you're interviewing at that moment. For example, you wouldn't interview with a small company and include "a giant corporation" as one of the criteria for evaluation. The interviewer would wonder why you had bothered to come to the interview since the company obviously couldn't meet that criteria. This could indicate that either you're someone who's so desperate that you're interviewing for anything, or you aren't paying any attention to what you're doing. Neither conclusion makes a good impression.

Example: "I want a stable company with a good reputation in the community, one that has a reputation for treating its employees fairly, and one that encourages promotion through the ranks."

When They Ask You If You Have Any Questions

At the end of the interview, the interviewer may offer you the opportunity to ask the questions. Many interviewers expect the applicant to ask questions, and if you simply say, "No," when they ask if you have questions, it does two things: it immediately ends the interview, and it causes the interviewer to wonder why you don't have any questions. He or she may misinterpret your lack of questions as a lack of interest. Your goal is to ask intelligent questions that demonstrate your interest as well as your ability to analyze the situation. However, you wouldn't want to ask a question about something already covered in the interview, unless it was a matter of clarification.

Don't discuss the salary, benefits package, vacation time, etc., unless you receive a job offer at the end of the interview. The interviewer will usually bring up those subjects prior to, or at the time of, making a job offer.

Typical questions you can ask at the end of the interview include the following:

96. *What opportunity for training would I have in this position?*
This lets the interviewer know that you're interested in learning more than just what's required at the moment.

97. *When would my first performance evaluation take place and how often do you conduct performance evaluations?*

This tells the interviewer that you expect evaluations, and that in fact you look forward to the opportunity to hear how the company views your performance.

98. *Please describe a typical day on the job.*

This indicates to the interviewer your continued interest in understanding the job requirements, and also gives you additional information to use in deciding whether this job is the right one for you if you receive a job offer.

99. *Is there a dress code?*

While a company's dress code may not be something you can't live with, you do need to be aware of such a code before you become an employee. The interviewer will see this as a practical and logical question, unless you relax too much and make an unfortunate remark such as, "Oh, no, you mean I'd have to dress up every day?"

100. *How would you describe this company's management style?*

This question lets the interviewer know that you have enough business experience to understand that different companies do have different management styles. It also gives you information you need in your evaluation of the merits of working for the company, should a job offer be forthcoming.

Additional Reading

Campbell, Colin. *Jobscape: Career Survival in the New Global Economy.* Indianapolis, IN: JIST Works, 1998.

Corcodilos, Nick A. *Ask the Headhunter—Reinventing the Interview to Win the Job.* New York, NY: Penguin, 1997.

DeLuca, Matthew J., *Best Answers to the 201 Most Frequently Asked Interview Questions.* New York, NY: McGraw-Hill, 1997.

Drake, John D. *The Perfect Interview—How to Get the Job You Really Want, 2nd Edition.* New York, NY: AMACOM, 1997.

Edwards, Paul and Sarah. *Finding Your Perfect Work.* New York, NY: G.P. Putnam's Sons, 1996.

Elkart, Martin. *Getting from Fired to Hired.* New York, NY: Macmillan General Reference—A Simon & Schuster Macmillan Company, 1997.

Eyler, David R. *Job Interviews that Mean Business, 2nd Edition.* New York, NY: Random House, 1996.

Farr, J. Michael. *America's Top Jobs for People Without College Degrees.* Indianapolis IN: JIST Works, 1997.

Fein, Richard. *101 Dynamite Questions to Ask at Your Job Interview.* Manassas Park, VA: Impact Publications, 1996.

Fein, Richard. *101 Dynamite Ways to Ace Your Job Interview.* Manassas Park, VA: Impact Publications, 1996.

Field, Shelly. *100 Best Careers for the 21st Century.* New York, NY: Macmillan General Reference—A Simon & Schuster Macmillan Company, 1996.

Fishman, Stephen. *Hiring Independent Contractors.* Berkeley, CA: Nolo Press, 1997.

Grappo, Gary Joseph. *The Top 10 Fears of Job Seekers.* New York, NY: The Berkeley Publishing Group, 1996.

Green, Paul, Ph.D. *Get Hired!—Winning Strategies to Ace the Interview.* Austin, TX: Bard Press, 1996.

Haft, Tim, Meg Heenehan, Marci Taub, and Michelle Tullier, Ph.D. *Job-Smart—What You Need to Know to Get the Job You Want.* New York, NY: Random House, 1997.

Hartman, Julia. *Strategic Job Jumping—How to Get from Where You Are to Where You Want to Be.* Rocklin, CA: Prima Publishing, 1997.

Hirsch, Arlene, S. *National Business Employment Weekly, 2nd Edition.* New York, NY: John Wiley & Sons, Inc., 1996.

Ireland, Susan. *The Complete Idiot's Guide to the Perfect Cover Letter.* New York, NY: Alpha Books—A Division of Macmillan Reference USA, 1997.

Krannich, Caryl Rae and Ronald L., Ph.D.s. *Interview for Success, Sixth Edition.* Manassas Park, VA: Impact Publications, 1997.

Marino, Kim. *Just Resumes—200 Powerful and Proven Successful Resumes to Get That Job.* New York, NY: John Wiley & Sons, 1997.

Moock, Theodore, R., Jr. *Get That Interview!* Hauppauge, NY: Barron's Educational Series, 1996.

Rogers, Roxanne S. *Get a Job You Love.* Chicago, IL: Dearborn Financial Publishing, 1996.

Rosse, Joseph. *High Impact Hiring.* San Francisco, CA: Jossey-Bass, 1997.

Schwartau, Winn and Chris Goggans. *The Complete Internet Business Tool Kit.* New York, NY: Van Nostrand Reinhold—A Division of International Thomson Publishing, 1996.

Shackelford, William G. *Minority Recruiting—Building the Strategies and Relationships for Effective Diversity Recruiting.* Dubuque, IA: Kendall/Hunt Publishing Company, 1996.

Troutman, Kathryn K. *The Federal Resume Guidebook.* Indianapolis, IN: JIST Works, 1997.

Witcher, Barbara Johnson. *Create the Job You Love.* Rocklin, CA: Prima Publishing, 1997.

Index

---

* Sample interview questions and answers, Appendix E.

---

* Sample interview questions and answers, Appendix E.

* Sample interview questions and answers, Appendix E.

* Sample interview questions and answers, Appendix E.

* Sample interview questions and answers, Appendix E.

* Sample interview questions and answers, Appendix E.

* Sample interview questions and answers, Appendix E.

---

* Sample interview questions and answers, Appendix E.

* Sample interview questions and answers, Appendix E.

* Sample interview questions and answers, Appendix E.

* Sample interview questions and answers, Appendix E.

* Sample interview questions and answers, Appendix E.

* Sample interview questions and answers, Appendix E.

* Sample interview questions and answers, Appendix E.

* Sample interview questions and answers, Appendix E.

* Sample interview questions and answers, Appendix E.

Tell me about your (or one of your) biggest
	accomplishments, 242*
Tell me about yourself, 219*
Tell me something you did that demonstrates
	your willingness to work hard, 252*
Tell me what is the worst thing you've heard
	concerning our company?, 236*
Temper, lost at work, 245*
Temporary
	jobs, 30, 62, 67, 68
	position, interview questions, 229–231*
	professional, 67
Terminated, 3
Termination
	jobless due to, xvii
	seeking employment due to, interview
		question, 226*
Terminology, industry to industry, 140
Tests
	answers, tip about, 150
	as part of interview process, 150
	pre-employment, 149–150
	vocational, 9, 10
Texas Workforce Commission, 207
Thank you letter, 153–154, see also Follow-up
	after
		informational interview, 70
		interview, 112, 151, 152
		meal, a, 169
	for time in reading resume, 46
	guidelines, 154
	Human Resources, 78
	job fairs, 80
	key tool in job search, 151
	three main sections, 153
	when networking, 87
Time, respect the, 78
Tips to help you remain positive, 4
Tip the scales, 152
Too old, 177
Track record, older candidate, 178
Training, 14, 24, 64
	opportunity for, 258*
Transferable skills, 14, 33, 140

Travel
	free to, 6
	interview questions about, 238–240*
Traveling
	benefit of, 240*
	question about, 142, 238–240*
Triad Job Search Network, 203
Turning Point Career Center, 194
Type of work, why think you would like,
	interview question, 223*
Typical day on job, 259*

U

Unemployed, 2, 3, 34, 71–73
Unemployment, 3
U.S. Department of Labor, on-line, 82
Unpaid internships, work experience, 44
Unprepared, for the interview, 180
Unwritten rules of behavior, 164
Upload, 191

V

Values, decision based on, 21
Video conference interview, 112, 115–117, see
	also Interview
Vocational tests, 9
Voice mail systems, for messages, 61
Volunteer
	organizations, networking, 61
	work, as work experience, 30, 44

W

Want to
	do, 7
	work here, why, 217*
Wardrobe, for the interview, 174, see also
	Dress, Interview
Washington Post, 83

* Sample interview questions and answers, Appendix E.

---

* Sample interview questions and answers, Appendix E.

* Sample interview questions and answers, Appendix E.